AUSTRIA

Sean Sheehan

MARSHALL CAVENDISH
New York • London • Sydney

Reference edition published 1993 by
Marshall Cavendish Corporation
2415 Jerusalem Avenue
P.O. Box 587
North Bellmore
New York 11710

© Times Editions Pte Ltd 1992

Originated and designed by
Times Books International, an imprint of
Times Editions Pte Ltd

Printed in Singapore

Library of Congress Cataloging-in-Publication Data:
Sheehan, Sean, 1951–
    Austria / Sean Sheehan : [illustrator, Kelvin Sim].
      p. cm.—(Cultures Of The World)
    Includes bibliographical references and index.
    Summary: Introduces the geography, history,
economy, culture, and people of Austria.
    ISBN 1-85435-454-X
    1. Austria—Juvenile literature [1. Austria.]
I. Sim, Kelvin, ill. II. Title. III. Series.
DB17.S44 1992
943.6—dc20   91–40515
             CIP
             AC

Cultures of the World

Editorial Director	Shirley Hew
Managing Editor	Shova Loh
Editors	Roseline Lum
	Goh Sui Noi
	June Khoo Ai Lin
	Siow Peng Han
	Leonard Lau
	Tan Kok Eng
	MaryLee Knowlton
Picture Editor	Yee May Kaung
Production	Edmund Lam
Design	Tuck Loong
	Ang Siew Lian
	Lee Woon Hong
	Lo Yen Yen
	Ong Su Ping
Illustrators	Suzana Fong
	Kelvin Sim
Cover Picture	Austrian Tourist Promotion Board

INTRODUCTION

THE NAME FOR AUSTRIA came from the German word *Österreich* meaning "Eastern Empire." Austria today is situated between Western and Eastern Europe and looks poised to play an important role in the emerging Europe of the 1990s.

Within the country itself, Austria is dominated by the famous Alps, a stunning snow-capped mountain range that covers almost three-quarters of the country. The Alpine peaks are breathtaking and year-round skiing is possible on some slopes, drawing in millions of tourists every year. Austria is equally famous for a rich artistic culture that has nurtured and inspired such great names as Mozart, Strauss and Schönberg.

This book, a part of the *Cultures of the World* series, provides insight into the lifestyles of the Austrians: their work, leisure, attitudes, beliefs, food and culture. It gives a glimpse of Austria that is more than what the average tourist sees.

CONTENTS

Sledging down the grassy slopes in summer.

CONTENTS

Skiing down the snow-white slopes in winter.

GEOGRAPHY

AUSTRIA HAS NO COASTLINE. It is surrounded on all sides by other countries: to the north lie Germany and Czechoslovakia and to the south Yugoslavia and Italy; in the east lies Hungary and in the west Switzerland and the tiny state of Liechtenstein.

The mountains known as the Alps cross Austria from east to west and dominate the southern and central parts of the country. Only in the north does the land flatten out into a plateau drained by the mighty Danube River that flows from the west.

The total area of landlocked Austria is 32,374 square miles, stretching 362 miles from east to west and 162 miles from north to south.

Opposite: **A peek at the peak—Grossglockner is the highest point in Austria.**

Below: **The Mieminger Plateau in Tyrol. A classic Austrian scene with mountains, trees, pasture and a castle.**

Above: **Valleys are fertile enough for farming.**

Below: **Many roads zig-zag up the mountains, making once isolated valley communities more accessible.**

THE ALPS

The most dramatic features of Austria's physical landscape are the mountains and foothills of the Alps where, above 6,000 feet, snow lies for six months of the year. On the higher peaks the snow never melts. The Alps dominate Austria and the plains make up less than 10% of the land. The mountains and hills are also rich in pasture land and the alluvial soils have enabled farmers to make their country almost self-sufficient when it comes to providing food.

The Alps were formed some 30 million years ago when tremendous disturbances deep in the earth caused powerful pressures to build up and fold large areas of rock into mountains. Geologists divide the Alps into three sections and all three may be found in Austria. The Northern Limestone Alps are the most inaccessible, with narrow peaks and barren areas of flat land. These mountains extend from the Tyrol up through the central parts of Salzburg to the Vienna Woods.

The central area of the Alps is made up of crystalline rocks, gneiss (pronounced "nice"), schists and granite, which over millions of years have weathered into spectacular shapes and sizes. Austria's highest and most famous mountain is the Grossglockner (12,457 feet) and a magnificent mountain road threads its way through this part of the Alps to provide tourists with a spectacular view of the mountain. The city of Innsbruck is situated on the margins of the Central Alps in the valley of the Inn River.

The Southern Limestone Alps jut into southern Austria from the north of Italy and are found south of the Drava River.

There are two important gaps in the mountains: one in the west that leads to Switzerland and the other one goes south to Italy. This southern route, known as the Brenner Pass, is very important because of its low-lying position. The winter snows never block the pass and so it remains open throughout the year. For centuries the Brenner Pass has provided the main route from Italy to Germany and nowadays roads and rail lines continue to link the two countries.

Glaciers move down the Alpine valleys like giant tongues of ice at Grossglockner

GLACIERS

A glacier is a large body of moving ice formed by conditions that are typically found in the Austrian Alps. In between the folds of the mountains the snow collects and thickens, compacting into ice as more snow piles up on top. When it is about 200 feet thick the lower layers of ice become plastic and start to move very slowly down the valley path. It moves like a giant but incredibly slow earthmover, scraping and grooving the bedrock of the valley floor and making the original fold between the mountains larger and deeper. The result, a U-shaped glacial valley, is a typical feature of the Austrian landscape and most of the country's rural villages and small towns are tucked into these valleys.

At the head of a glacier valley, where the original depression formed the origin of the glacier, the effect of the ice pulling down rock is the carving of a bowl-like hollow from the face of the mountain. Known as cirques, it is sometimes the case that two cirques form almost side by side and all that is left of the original mountain is a narrow ridge, called an *arête*. This is what accounts for the slender but huge mountains found in the Alps of Austria and neighboring countries.

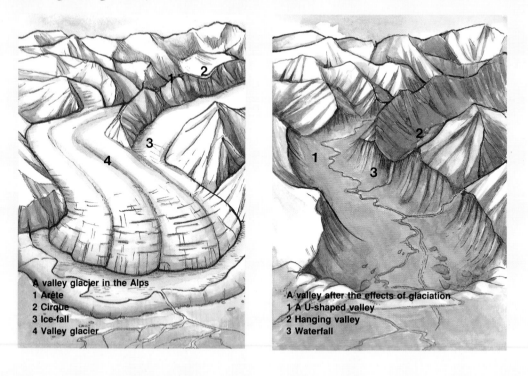

A valley glacier in the Alps
1 Arête
2 Cirque
3 Ice-fall
4 Valley glacier

A valley after the effects of glaciation
1 A U-shaped valley
2 Hanging valley
3 Waterfall

A winter scene at Bad Hofgastein.

CLIMATE

In the winter months temperatures drop to between 20 F and 30 F, and in the mountain areas it gets even colder, especially at night. Throughout the winter the valleys are often filled with fog and cold air fills the sheltered valleys facing south, making them colder than the slopes above. The mountain villages have clean and warmer air so the sport resorts operate at all times. Come summertime the temperatures move up to between 65 F and 75 F.

The *foehn* (also spelled *föhn*) is the name of a warm and dry wind that affects life in some parts of Austria. In the United States the same kind of wind in the Rocky Mountains and High Sierras is sometimes called the *chinook*. It is formed by the compression of air as it comes down from the mountains. The effect is to raise the local temperature. These winds can be beneficial for farmers who can take advantage of higher temperatures than would normally be expected for high altitudes. The disadvantage is the danger of avalanches due to a rise in temperature. The snow melts gradually, but there comes a point when quite suddenly the snow and ice may shift and fall down the mountainside. These sudden movements, known as avalanches, pose an immediate danger to anyone caught below one of them. Big avalanches can block off roads and cut off small mountain communities for long periods of time.

11

Wild flowers in the mountains. Due to the short growing season, harsh winters and strong winds, mountain flowers are usually stunted and much shorter than their counterparts in the plains.

FLORA AND FAUNA

The characteristic flora and fauna of Austria is a result of the country's Alpine climate. Up to about 4,000 feet the mountains of Austria support forests of deciduous trees like beech, birch and oak. Far more common nowadays, though, are forests of conifers like pine and larch and other conifers. Fir and spruce are able to grow on the thinner soils above 4,000 feet. Most of Austria's forests are privately owned businesses with the trees being systematically grown and cut down for purely commercial purposes.

The Alpine landscape has also produced colorful flowers that are not found elsewhere as they have adapted to habitats with low temperatures, strong winds and the seasonal snows. They are usually small and compact in size and the growing season is often a brief one with the flowers popping up soon after the snow melts. The small white edelweiss is a typical alpine flower, made famous by the song in *The Sound of Music*, sung by Christopher Plummer and Julie Andrews. Nowadays it is against the law to pick this highly protected flower.

Flora and Fauna

The most interesting animals to be found in Austria are fur-bearing ones. There are now strict conservation laws in operation because much of the animal life is in danger of extinction. The goat-like chamois is one of the elusive mountain-dwelling creatures, recognized by round, short horns that turn backward and downward at the top to form a hook. Its feet have cup-shaped depressions, specially adapted to the mountain terrain, that allow it to perch on ledges no larger than a person's hand. More common are the squirrel-like marmots that live in colonies, hibernating for many months. On waking in spring they mate and set about devouring farmers' vegetables. Other animals to be seen in Austria are foxes, wildcats and deer.

Alpine birds include the ptarmigan, rarely seen close up, which changes from a brown color in summer to pure white in winter. In the cold it crouches down and allows itself to be buried in the snow until the climate improves. A regular visitor to the Salzburg area is the griffon vulture from the Balkans. Despite a wingspan of 10 feet it is not commonly seen. Even rarer is the golden eagle which hunts in pairs over the same area for the whole of its life. The last wolf was killed in Austria over 50 years ago and bears are no longer seen.

At one time there were over 70 different species of fish in the Danube but the pollution of the river, within Austria and the neighboring countries, is destroying the rich diversity of fish life. It is only a matter of time before wonders like the giant catfish, measuring up to 13 feet, are no longer found.

Below: **The goat-like chamois. In ancient times the fur of the chamois was used to line clothing in the winter.**

Bottom: **The squirrel-like marmot. It is often hunted by large birds of prey.**

13

Above: **A cruise boat brings tourists down the Danube River. The Wachau Valley provides glimpses of castle ruins, vineyards and orchards.**

Opposite: **Although highly polluted in certain stretches, the Danube is still a source of good, clean fun.**

THE DANUBE

The Danube is a mighty river 1,770 miles long, starting in Germany and emptying into the Black Sea in Romania. Over 2,000 years ago the Romans used the river as a northern frontier to their empire and it was while navigating the river that they founded Vienna, now the capital of Austria. Nearly all the country's other rivers flow into the Danube. On its journey through Austria, the Danube's character changes according to the land around it.

When the river enters Austria from Germany the scenery is a dramatic one because the river valley narrows and deep forests or sheer cliffs loom up on either side. The river here drops at the rate of three feet for every one mile and the resulting turbulence made it notoriously difficult to navigate in the days before boats were motorized.

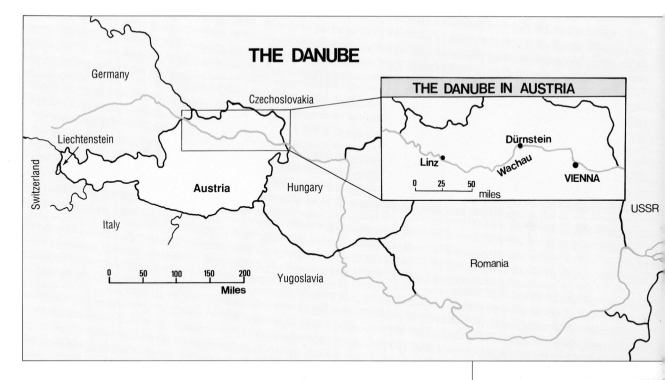

THE DANUBE

Germany

Czechoslovakia

Liechtenstein

Switzerland

Austria

Hungary

Italy

0   50   100   150   200
Miles

Yugoslavia

Romania

USSR

THE DANUBE IN AUSTRIA

Dürnstein

Linz

Wachau

VIENNA

0   25   50
miles

After the city of Linz, however, the landscape becomes less wild and more picturesque as the river enters the Wachau Valley. On the banks the bare rocks seem to soften into hills where the dark forests give way to vineyards and orchards. Medieval castles perched on the slopes add to the romantic atmosphere of the river.

As the river approaches Vienna it stretches out in swampy channels, but engineers have channeled the river through a canal for its actual passage through the city. If Johann Strauss Jr. were composing his famous waltz *The Blue Danube* today, he might have called it *The Brown Danube* instead—such is the pollution from city factories!

After Vienna the Danube flows into the great plains of Czechoslovakia and Hungary and continues for hundreds of miles through Yugoslavia, Romania and finally to the Black Sea. This part of Europe has never been as highly developed as Western Europe and the Iron Curtain that divided the communist countries from the capitalist ones helped make Vienna the geographical and political frontier of the Western world.

HISTORY

THE EARLIEST TRACES of human life in Austria are the remains of Neanderthal man, people who lived through the last Ice Age, and who some 30,000 years ago, disappeared from the face of Europe. Whether they just reached an evolutionary dead end and became extinct or evolved into modern man is still an unresolved controversy. If they were supplanted by modern people migrating into Europe from Africa via the Middle East, as many scholars believe, it is very likely the new people entered Europe and Austria along the valley of the Danube River.

The Danube Valley became a recognized route from Eastern to Western Europe bringing travelers through Austria. The Brenner Pass was a safe and sure way of moving south through the Alps, especially in the winter months. A natural meeting place developed where traders going south to Rome or Alexandria met traders moving east to west.

A settlement grew up on the banks of the Danube that later became known as *Wien* (Vienna). This was the beginning of an Austria that would develop into a powerful empire lasting over 600 years only to suddenly collapse after World War I. Today, Austria's importance is again due to its unique location between east and west as the old Communist Europe, which was locked in on itself, turns westward.

Opposite: **In the armory at Graz, body armor, muskets and cannons were kept ready for battle against the Turks in the 17th century.**

Below: **Vienna, situated along the Danube River, was the meeting place for travelers from both Eastern and Western Europe.**

Vienna by the banks of the Danube River. Metternich, the wily Austrian statesman of the 19th century, once said, "Eastwards from Vienna, the Orient begins."

THE CELTS AND THE ROMANS

The Celts were a fierce group of people who shared a common language and a culture distinguished by a gift for craftsmanship. In the year 390 B.C., they sacked Rome and around the same time invaded Austria, where they continued to exert an influence for over 300 years. They brought into Austria their technical skills and a love of art which can still be discerned in the Austrian character. It was the Celts who first opened up the copper and salt mines and the earliest village on the site of Vienna was occupied by the Celts.

Somewhere around 30 B.C., the Celts were displaced by the Romans, although the legionaries of Rome had explored the Danube long before that. In fact, they came to the conclusion that the great river was the best place to dig in against the wandering barbarian tribes from Germany that constantly threatened their empire. They fortified the Celtic village on the banks of the river that would later become Vienna and named it Vindobona.

As in many other parts of Europe, the Romans built strong roads and established laws that laid the foundations for the development of commerce and civic life. The Roman emperor and philosopher Marcus Aurelius spent a lot of time in Austria trying to consolidate a firm defense against the tribes of northern Europe and he died in Vienna in A.D. 180.

INVASIONS FROM GERMANY AND HUNGARY

Roughly from the 4th century to the year 1000 the land of Austria (still not known or understood as a separate country in our sense of the word) was settled and fought over by a bewildering range of tribes from Germany in the north and from Hungary in the east.

Salzburg Cathedral—a glorious result of European missionary zeal.

It is difficult to chronicle these centuries because written records are scarce and the invading tribes were diverse in nature. Their legacy seems minimal compared to the impact of Christianity that was, around the same time, making itself felt in this part of Europe. Missionaries from countries like Ireland spread their beliefs and established their churches. In the year 774 a cathedral was erected in the town of Salzburg, now one of Austria's larger cities.

The tribes from the east in Hungary, known as Magyars, made continual raids into the Austrian Danube Valley and were a constant threat to Charlemagne's empire, formed by Germanic tribes after the breakup of the Roman Empire. In fact, it was during Charlemagne's rule that Austrian territory was christened the "Eastern Kingdom" because it was seen as the easternmost extent of his influence. The German word for "Eastern Empire" is *Österreich*, which is the origin of the name Austria. It was Otto the Great, a German who founded the Holy Roman Empire, who finally managed to deal a decisive blow to the Magyars in the year 955. After that the Magyars settled down in the plains of Hungary and Austria began to develop as an independent society.

Hochosterwitz Castle—a fortified limestone outcrop in Carinthia used as a defense post against invaders.

THE FIRST ROYAL FAMILY

Austria's first royal family was the Babenbergs, a group of German nobles who were originally given the land around Vienna but who extended their domain to cover much of what is now called Austria. Their rule lasted some 300 years and accounts for much of what is now typically Austrian: the German language, the scores of castles that tourists photograph on their boat trips along the Danube (or even spend a night in, for many of these castles have now been converted into hotels), the vineyards, and the monasteries such as the Cistercian settlement at Heiligenstadt.

It was during the time of the Babenbergs that Vienna became firmly established as the capital city and it flourished, the legend has it, because of the huge supply of money it obtained from ransoming the English king, Richard the Lion-Hearted.

RICHARD THE LION-HEARTED

It was toward the end of the Babenberg rule, in the late 12th century, that the Third Crusade took place. The Crusades were a violent struggle between European states and those in the Middle East for control of valuable trade routes through the Middle East. The Crusades were conducted as a religious war between Christianity and Islam. During the Third Crusade the Duke of Austria quarreled with the English king, Richard I, known as Richard the Lion-Hearted. When Richard was returning to England after the Crusade he tried to pass through Austria in disguise, but was discovered and held prisoner by the Duke in Dürnstein Castle, overlooking the Danube. While Richard lay prisoner in Austria, his half brother John was ruling unjustly in England, opposed by the legendary Robin Hood of Sherwood forest, a staunch ally of Richard the Lion-Hearted.

The story has it that Richard's faithful minstrel, Blondel, searched everywhere for his king, singing beneath every castle wall he could find. Eventually he reached Dürnstein where Richard recognized Blondel's singing and signaled to his minstrel. This led to Richard's eventual release, after the payment of a large ransom, and his triumphant return to England.

Statue of Empress Maria Theresa. The empress brought great prosperity to the Hapsburg dynasty with her reforms in the 18th century.

THE HAPSBURG EMPIRE

Enjoying one of the longer reigns in world history, the Hapsburg family ruled Austria and large areas of Europe from 1282 to the end of World War I in 1918. The Hapsburgs started as landowners and, through a series of diplomatic marriages, built up an empire that stretched from Spain to Hungary.

It was the Turks who put up the strongest resistance to the Austrian Empire. In the 16th century, they almost captured Vienna, only to be pushed back from the city walls and eventually defeated.

The Austrian Empire of the Hapsburgs was so extensive and wealthy that there were many wars fought over it. The Thirty Years' War from 1618 to 1648 was one, and another important one was the War of the Austrian Succession that led to the emperor's oldest daughter, Maria Theresa, ruling the empire. Other power groups which wanted the territories for themselves fought Maria Theresa on the grounds that a woman could not inherit her father's kingdom. Visitors to Austria today can view some of the palaces built by the Hapsburgs.

THE END OF THE AUSTRIAN EMPIRE

The beginning of the end came when a weakened Austrian Empire agreed to share power with its former subject, Hungary. This arrangement may have suited the rulers but it did little to satisfy the Slavs of Eastern Europe who now found themselves ruled by German-speaking Austrians and the Magyars of Hungary. When a Slav nationalist assassinated the heir to the Austrian throne in 1914, the event sparked off World War I. The underlying cause of World War I was a struggle between European nations for economic supremacy and, when Austria found itself on the losing side in 1918, its lucrative empire was divided among the victors. A new Austria, one-eighth of its former size, was declared a republic for the first time.

Suddenly the people of Austria, like their neighbors in Germany who were also on the losing side, found themselves economically very weak. The two countries wanted to unite but the victors would not allow this. As the Great Depression of 1929 gathered pace a young man in Austria found an explanation for his country's ills. Vienna, before 1918, had been the capital of a cosmopolitan empire of 35 million people; it was now the capital of a small and impoverished republic with a population of 7 million—all German speaking. The young man, who soon left for Germany, blamed the Jews for everything that was going wrong and he had a plan for putting things right. His name was Adolf Hitler.

"We shall destroy you and wipe all traces of unbelievers off the face of the earth. Regardless of age, we shall put all of you through excruciating tortures before we kill you."
— Turkish ultimatum to the people of Vienna in 1683

The Schloss Schönbrunn was the summer palace of the Hapsburgs. The design and decorations have remained as they were since the time of Empress Maria Theresa.

ADOLF HITLER (1889–1945)

Adolf Hitler, the German dictator, was born and brought up in Austria. He embraced the anti-Semitism that was common in Austria and Central Europe at the time and would later write of Vienna, "Wherever I went I began to see Jews, and the more I saw, the more sharply they became distinguished in my eyes from the rest of humanity...gradually I began to hate them."

In Germany he built up his Nazi Party and invaded Austria in 1938, a year before the outbreak of World War II. At the time, the takeover was accepted by the other European powers. It was another year before England was forced to declare war, having realized that Hitler intended to rebuild the Hapsburg Empire with himself as emperor.

Hitler and his party were determined to wipe out the entire Jewish people and they began a process of extermination with camps being established across Europe equipped with gas chambers for systematic slaughter. When Hitler's Nazis ruled Austria they built such a camp near the village of Mauthausen on the Danube. More than 30,000 Jews were murdered in this camp and visitors to Austria today can visit the site of the camp and its grisly remains. It is estimated that 4 million Jews died in these camps across Europe and perhaps a million more died in ghettos of starvation and disease. Over a million were shot by special killing squads and by the end of the war, in Austria alone, over 160,000 Jews were dead.

NEUTRAL AUSTRIA

After World War II Austria was occupied by the four major nations that had defeated Nazi Germany—the United States, Britain, France and the Soviet Union. In 1955 Austria became fully independent and the country was determined to remain neutral and free. Although Austria has recently applied to join the Economic Community (EC) of Western European nations, it has always refused to join the military organization, NATO, that most of those countries belong to. Austria is also committed to never possessing nuclear weapons.

In 1989 Hungary began to dismantle the barbed wire fences and the electronic alarm system along the 150-mile border with Austria. Hungary also allowed East Germans to travel through Hungary to reach West Germany. This historic event eventually led to the dismantling of the Berlin Wall and the consequent unification of Germany. When the East Germans were flowing through Hungary, the government of Austria provided important transit aid.

In 1990 and 1991 the collapse of communism in Eastern Europe set in motion a huge wave of European migration and Austria was swamped by massive waves of East Europeans seeking new lives in the West. Toward the end of 1990 Austria had to send troops to its border with Hungary because large numbers of Romanians were slipping in through the woods. Austria was awarded the 1989 Humanitarian Award by a Jewish refugee organization in acknowledgement of the transit aid given over the years to nearly 300,000 Soviet Jews. In fact, since 1945 Austria has taken in some 2 million East Europeans out of whom some half a million have stayed in the country. Now, it seems, Austria cannot take any more and during the 1990 general election, one party gained support by calling for stringent limits to any further immigration.

GOVERNMENT

FOR THE FIRST 50 YEARS of this century government in Austria was in a perpetual state of change and disorder. Conflict and disagreement were bitter and violent, and politics were characterized by a deep split between the conservative forces of the countryside, where the Catholic Church was all-powerful, and the socialist groups in the cities that demanded change and reform. This was the background to a virtual civil war that broke out in the 1930s and the eventual takeover of Austria by Nazi Germany.

Opposite: **The Parliament Building in Vienna.**

Below: **The City Hall in Vienna is a Flemish Gothic guildhall.**

After World War II, as Austria began to rebuild its identity as an independent country, there was a new spirit of cooperation that was determined to avoid the conflicts of the past. Government in Austria in the second half of this century has been the very opposite of what it once was. Nowadays, Austria is famous for political stability and consensus. Different political parties work together to share the task of government and, compared to some other European countries, political life in Austria is dull but very safe. The controversy over President Waldheim is the only political incident in Austria since the end of World War II that has become international news.

GOVERNMENT STRUCTURE

Austria is a democratic republic and a federation, a union of nine provinces, with two houses of parliament: the Federal Council and the National Council. Of the two, the National Council is the more important. Any bill, except the budget, must be approved by the Federal Council, but if it should veto a bill, the National Council can override this veto by a simple majority vote. The Federal Council is made up of representatives from each of the nine states whereas the National Council, as the name implies, represents the country as a whole.

One interesting feature of the constitution is that it allows for any bill to be put before parliament for approval if it can show the support of at least 400,000 citizens. This allows for petitions to be put before parliament that do not necessarily originate from one of the main parties.

The president of Austria is elected by all citizens, for a period of six years, and the president acts as head of state, appoints the cabinet and, in theory at least, is the commander-in-chief of the armed forces. In reality, the president is more of a figurehead and usually follows the suggestions of the chancellor when it comes to important decisions. The chancellor is like a prime minister, the leader of the government.

According to the constitution, the state of Austria is committed to perpetual neutrality. As such the country has never belonged to NATO (the North Atlantic Treaty Organization), the military expression of Western Europe's opposition to the power of the USSR. Austria may have a new role to play in the light of the political developments in Europe today.

THE CONTROVERSIAL PRESIDENT

Kurt Waldheim was elected president of Austria in 1986. He was already an international figure, having served as Secretary General of the United Nations, but as president of Austria he achieved notoriety because of revelations and allegations concerning his past.

During the election campaign critics pointed to his war record and his alleged membership in a Nazi organization. More damning was the allegation that he was involved in Nazi atrocities in the Balkans committed against Slavs taken as prisoners by the Nazis.

After his election the criticisms and allegations were strengthened as researchers dug into war records which appeared to support many of the charges. Waldheim himself refused to admit that he had anything to be ashamed of. In 1988 the United States put him on their list of undesirable aliens and the Austrian president faced international isolation. Political groups within the country called for his resignation.

A commission of international historians was established to try and resolve the controversy and they came to the conclusion that, while there was no proof of Waldheim's personal guilt, he had nevertheless been fully aware of the Nazi atrocities committed in the Balkans. This was something Waldheim had always denied and even after the commission's report was published, he still refused to resign.

Waldheim's presidency comes to an end in 1992, but the way Waldheim received widespread support within Austria for his position rekindled the anti-Semitism of the past. A public opinion poll, even before the controversy arose, suggested that 25% of Austrians were strongly anti-Semitic; and only 15% of those questioned claimed to have no such prejudice.

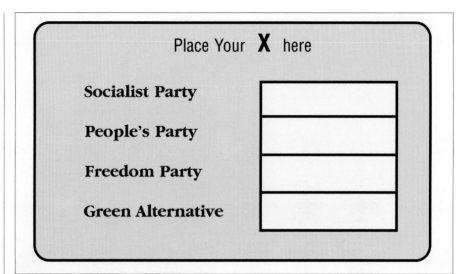

Place Your **X** here

Socialist Party

People's Party

Freedom Party

Green Alternative

Most supporters of the Socialist Party live in the cities.

WHOM DO AUSTRIANS VOTE FOR?

Austria is a democracy and the citizens vote every four years for a new government.

The Socialist Party receives most of its votes from the Austrians who live and work in the cities and large towns. The party has close links with the trade unions. The People's Party receives its main support from the countryside and is closely associated with the Catholic Church. These are the two major parties and most Austrians vote for one or the other. Regularly, each party receives around 45% of the total votes and this means that neither party finds it easy to form a government that can rule effectively on its own. In practice, the two parties form a coalition and share the important posts.

Unlike some countries, where such coalitions never seem to last long and political rivalries are bitter and prolonged, the system in Austria works surprisingly well and Austria's citizens are largely content with shared governments. And the consensus works: the economy is strong and reliable and unemployment is kept low. The new independent countries of Eastern Europe, as well as many Western nations, are envious of such economic stability and prosperity.

The other two main parties in Austria have very little in common with each other. The Freedom Party is very right-wing and strongly opposed to any government help for the disadvantaged. Although any self-proclaimed Nazi party is illegal in Austria (the only kind of party that is forbidden), many critics have accused the Freedom Party of being supported by the sort of people who once supported Hitler.

The newest party gaining support in Austria is the Green Party. Green parties are forming all over Europe and what they have in common is a concern for the environment and the need for legislation to safeguard people and their environment rather than the interests of capital and the profit motive.

Support for the People's Party comes mainly from the Church and from the people living in the countryside.

AUSTRIA AND HUMAN RIGHTS

Austria has a very good record for human rights. According to *The Economist*'s World Human Rights Record, Austria's record serves as an example to the rest of the world:

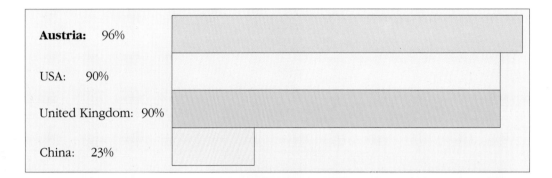

Austria: 96%	
USA: 90%	
United Kingdom: 90%	
China: 23%	

Such a high rating is based on the country's guaranteed freedoms, for example, the right to publish in an ethnic language, the right to abstain from compulsory religious education in schools, the right of workers to go on strike, a free press and so on.

Austria is a very free, yet orderly, country. After the hardships and horrors during World War II and the struggle for stability after the war, fighting, rioting and strikes are viewed as counter-productive and unwelcome.

THE 1990 GENERAL ELECTION

Before the 1990 election Austrians had a coalition government. After the election they still had one. So has much changed? Not really, except that the Socialists increased their strength by one seat and the People's Party lost 17 seats.

The seats that the mildly conservative People's Party lost went to the very right-wing Freedom Party. Before the election the Freedom Party called for the need to restrict immigration from countries like Romania to the east of Austria, suggesting that they were taking Austrians' jobs and houses. The coalition continues with the Socialists being the strongest partner led by Franz Vranitzky. Because coalitions have become so common in Austria, with just minor variations after each election, one newspaper headlined Franz Vranitzky's victory "Waltzing Vranitzky." (The Vienna Waltz is a three-step waltz, characterized by slow formal steps and the partners close together.)

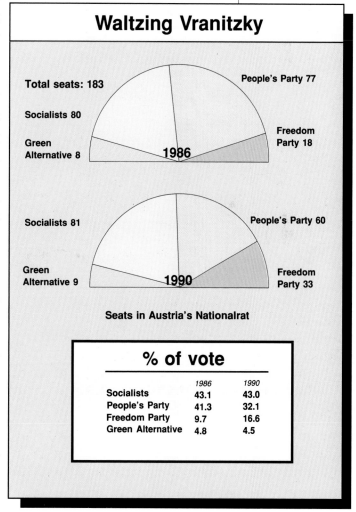

Waltzing Vranitzky

Total seats: 183

Socialists 80

Green Alternative 8

1986

People's Party 77

Freedom Party 18

Socialists 81

Green Alternative 9

1990

People's Party 60

Freedom Party 33

Seats in Austria's Nationalrat

% of vote

	1986	1990
Socialists	43.1	43.0
People's Party	41.3	32.1
Freedom Party	9.7	16.6
Green Alternative	4.8	4.5

ECONOMY

AUSTRIA'S ECONOMY IS STRONG and well-balanced; agriculture and industry are both firmly established and an indication of the country's economic well-being can be seen from the fact that Austria has been able to sustain its economic growth without joining the Economic Community (EC) of which so many other European states are members. Austria has now applied to join the EC and it is only a matter of time before acceptance as a member is warmly given. Austria's low inflation rate, always below 5%, is the envy of many countries and the trade unions work closely with the government to minimize industrial unrest.

Opposite: **Boating on the lake in St. Wolfgang. Not only the mountains but also the lakes attract both local and foreign visitors.**

Below: **A commercial street and plaza in Graz, Austria's second largest city. Population trends show a drift from the countryside to the cities for employment.**

Part of the Silvretta Dam in Vorarlberg. Since World War II, Austria has become one of Europe's foremost producers of hydroelectric power.

INDUSTRY

Most of Austria's industrial strength is a result of natural resources. Industry is centered around Vienna and its industrial suburbs, where 25% of the population live and work. Other manufacturing areas are to be found near large towns, like Graz, the second largest city in Austria, and important supplies of iron ore provide the basis of industrial life in Styria.

Extensive programs of reconstruction and development in industries such as hydroelectric power, oil, natural gas, mining, heavy industry, textiles and chemical engineering were carried out after World War II. The benefit is a prosperous and fairly stable economy. The cost is a change in national character and tradition as more people—especially the younger generation—move out of the countryside to the cities in search of employment.

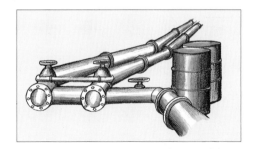

1

2

INDUSTRY

3

1. Austria exports its electricity to Germany, Italy and Switzerland.

2. After Romania and Germany, Austria is the largest producer of crude oil in Europe.

3. Austria is the world's largest supplier of magnesite. It is used in the car manufacturing industry.

4. Steel is made from iron, and valuable deposits of iron ore are found in Styria.

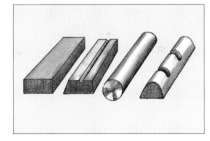

4

5. Salt is still being mined today in mines discovered by the Celts 2,000 years ago.

6. Traditional crafts like glassmaking and woodcarving are still practiced.

6

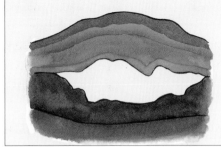

5

A corn harvest—harvesting is still done by hand on mountain farms because the slopes are too steep for machines.

AGRICULTURE

A large proportion of the cultivated land is given over to forestry with conifers such as spruce being systematically planted, allowed to mature and then cut down for commercial use. Reforestation is going on all the time so there is little left of the original primeval forest that once carpeted so much of Central Europe. A lot of the timber is not processed within the country but exported as untreated lumber. What is processed is turned into paper for export.

Most of Austria's farms are small and family-run. Over 80% of farms cultivate less than 50 acres of land and around 40% work fewer than 12 acres. Well over half of the farms are part-time concerns with tourism being a major subsidiary source of income. Unfortunately, it is only in the tourist areas that farmers can rent out rooms or act as mountain guides or ski instructors. In the eastern border areas adjacent to Czechoslovakia, Hungary and Yugoslavia—despite the good land—there is little tourist trade and the farming population is decreasing all the time.

A special feature of farming in Austria is the mountain farm. Austria has the highest proportion of mountain farms in Europe. Unfortunately this form of farming is declining because modern machinery cannot work on the steep slopes and labor is attracted to the tourist trade. Government subsidies are given to Alpine farmers in an attempt to preserve mountain farming and the cultural landscape in the Alps.

Austria grows more than three-quarters of its own food. Crop and fruit farming are not entirely feasible in all farming areas but grass and clover grow well. Therefore most Alpine farmers are dairy farmers. There are even pipelines to carry milk from highland farms to points below in the valleys.

Nearly all farmers own cattle in Austria. The cows graze on the grass and clover that grow so well in the pastures.

Above: **People on a pulley in Kirchdorf. The ski resorts in Austria attract thousands of tourists each year.**

Opposite: **A stork and its nest in Burgenland. Conservation programs to preserve the natural grassland and wetlands in the east of Austria have led to the protection of many migrant and breeding wetland birds.**

TOURISM—A BLESSING OR A BLIGHT?

Tourism is vitally important to Austria's economy. In 1986 visitors to the country spent over $6 billion and the number of visitors each year is around 13 million. This is remarkable for a country of less than 8 million people.

The mountain resorts attract visitors year-round. The majority of tourists are from Germany, probably attracted by the common language, and the Netherlands. There are three main cities that attract tourists: Innsbruck, beautifully situated amid mountains; Salzburg, with its internationally famed music festivals and romantic architecture; and Vienna, the country's capital. Once the residential and political center of the Hapsburg dynasty, the city of Vienna is famous for its many old buildings.

Only some parts of Austria are really popular with tourists: the western provinces of Tyrol, Salzburg and Carinthia, and Vienna itself. The effect of tourism can be seen in the way new houses are built in the western provinces. An extra floor will be added for the purpose of renting rooms to visitors.The price to pay for such large scale tourism is the change, some would say destruction, of the social structure of valley life. Some people believe customs and traditions are trivialized once they become marketable and the cultural meaning is lost.

THREATS TO THE ENVIRONMENT

Alongside the large forests of commercial trees, which are systematically planted only to be later cut down, Austria still possesses the largest primeval riverine forest in the whole of Europe. It is the 19,760-acre Hainburg Forest. At present there are plans to construct a huge hydroelectric plant on the Danube River near this forest and the building of the dam would destroy 1,976 acres of the forest and prevent the annual spring flooding of the rest of the forest. Supporters of the project argue that the hydroelectric plant would result in a reduction of the number of fossil-fueled power stations and thus there would be less acid rain pollution. Critics of the dam argue that if the Danube ceases to flow through the forest, and be purified by it, then there will be pollution of the groundwater that Vienna depends on.

In 1986 Austria experienced severe contamination by radioactive fallout following the Chernobyl nuclear reactor disaster. Thousands of tons of food had to be destroyed. The Chernobyl disaster also settled the controversy over the future of Austria's Zwentendorf nuclear plant. This plant had been completed in 1978 but it never went into operation because of the opposition within Austria to nuclear power. After Chernobyl the argument was settled and the plant was dismantled piece by piece and sold to anyone who wanted spare parts for a nuclear power station.

Plans to build a large nuclear reprocessing plant in neighboring Bavaria, in Germany, continue to meet with opposition not only within Germany but also from Austria. Any leaks or damage to such a plant would affect Austrians just as much as it would Germans.

AUSTRIANS

A SURE WAY TO OFFEND an Austrian is to assume that, since Austria is so close to Germany and the Austrians speak German all the time, Austrians are sort of Germans really. "No!" would be the reaction of an outraged Austrian, who is proud of his country's independent identity and who is acutely aware of *not* being German.

An Austrian would be equally offended if one made a different kind of assumption, namely that all Austrians are basically the same. "No!" would be the equally spirited reply. A Viennese would claim to be as different from a native of Vorarlberg as night is from day, and an inhabitant of Vorarlberg would readily agree. Yet they would both categorically assert that they are Austrians.

Opposite: **A little boy in Lederhosen.**

Left: **People in a park. The people of Austria are not homogeneous because of their colorful political history.**

A couple in a park. The people of a particular region are sometimes more similar to people in neighboring countries than they are to their fellow Austrians from another region.

Austria is a federation and most of the nine states have a distinct personality of their own. As a result the people of each state tend to be different and so there is really no typical Austrian as such. The most important factor that accounts for the differences in various provinces is

Austria's proximity to so many neighboring countries and their cultures. This closeness has given rise to population shifts and consequent cultural "invasions," the legacies of which largely determine the interesting differences between one part of Austria and another. The physical geography of Austria has also influenced the country's cultural development because the Alps have created physical barriers between one area and another. Such cultural differences can exist even between one valley community and another just a few miles away, manifesting themselves in differences of costume and dialect. As a result, some Austrians are more like the people in neighboring countries than their fellow Austrians.

THE PEOPLE OF BURGENLAND

Burgenland is the least visited part of Austria, as far as tourists from Western Europe are concerned. Its closeness to Hungary has produced a people who are more subject to the influence of that country than any other part of Austria. Burgenland is one of the only two parts of Austria where German is not spoken by everyone. The state has an important Croatian minority and Croat is the preferred language for these people.

Historically, the people of Burgenland have closer links with Hungary than any other part of Austria. After the breakup of the Austro-Hungarian empire after World War I, a plebiscite (a vote by which people of a political unit determine autonomy or affiliation with another country) was held . The result of the vote was that this slice of Hungary became a part of Austria.

Burgenland doesn't look like the postcard-picture Austria because there are no snowy mountains and the people are mostly fruit and vegetable farmers. Therefore, the people of Burgenland face two related economic problems.

Their lifestyle is subject to seasonal variation. Agricultural production is profitable in the spring and summer but not so during the winter months. Moreover, they do not have the benefit of tourism to supplement their income, although the nature reserve around Lake Neusiedl—a steppe lake with wide reed belts—is attracting many visitors because of the great number of wetland birds breeding there. As a consequence there has been a population drift away from Burgenland toward Vienna and other parts of the country.

Father and son horse-taxi drivers. Not all who work in the city were born there; many came from the countryside to seek employment.

45

Above: **A farmhouse in Styria. Food is produced for consumption *within* the region in Styria.**

Opposite: **A Tyrolean farmer drives his horse cart through the village. Traditional means of transportation are still used in the countryside.**

THE PEOPLE OF STYRIA

The people of Styria live close to Yugoslavia, Hungary and Italy, a fact which might help explain their strong sense of independence. One writer recounted recently how he was enjoying a dinner in a farmhouse near Graz when he was surprised to discover that both the lamb he was eating and the wine he was drinking were local produce. He asked the farmer why such good quality meat and wine were not available in Vienna, where lamb is expensively imported from New Zealand. The farmer's serious reply was that in Styria farmers didn't export their lamb or their wines. The idea of selling their produce to their own country's capital is viewed in terms of international trade!

If not engaged in farming the people of Styria are likely to have jobs connected with one of the state's major industries: forestry, glass manufacturing or the magnesite and iron and steel industries. The center of the iron ore industry is the Erzberg (Brass Mountain), the largest open-cast working of iron ore in Europe. In recent years, however, the iron and steel industry has been in decline.

THE TYROLEANS

Tyrol is surrounded by majestic mountains and the people of this state are famous for their traditions and nationalist fervor. The Tyroleans are proud of the fact that they possess a rich heritage as free and independent farmers who were never serfs to the local nobility. Today, this history accounts for their confidence and strong sense of being Tyrolean and

Austrian. It is connected with the turbulent history of a province that has been fought over many times in history. The existence of once-precious silver mines plus the proximity of the Brenner Pass through the Alps to Italy made Tyrol a much disputed area. When the state was given to the king of Bavaria by Napoleon in the early 19th century, the Tyroleans rose in revolt under the leadership of Andreas Hofer and, after Hofer's execution, he became an important folk hero.

Tyrol is the part of Austria that nearly all tourists visit and Innsbruck, the major city of Tyrol, is the most historic and renowned city after Vienna. Surrounded by mountains and expressways, Innsbruck has a spectacular location and has twice been chosen as the site for the Winter Olympic Games. Tourism is vitally important for the people of Tyrol, many of whom earn their living as mountain guides and hoteliers.

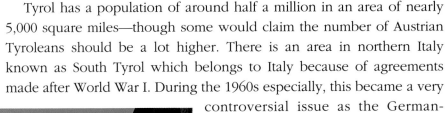

Scenic Innsbruck—with the old quarter in the foreground and the Alps in the back. Many Tyroleans work in the tourist industry.

Tyrol has a population of around half a million in an area of nearly 5,000 square miles—though some would claim the number of Austrian Tyroleans should be a lot higher. There is an area in northern Italy known as South Tyrol which belongs to Italy because of agreements made after World War I. During the 1960s especially, this became a very controversial issue as the German-speaking inhabitants of South Tyrol felt their Austrian heritage was not being properly recognized. Terrorist attacks took place at the time, although now South Tyrol has some degree of autonomy and the German language is accepted in this part of northern Italy. Still, it is not uncommon to find Tyroleans in Austria who possess property in South Tyrol and consider that part of Italy to be more legitimately a part of Austria.

Recently another kind of territorial dispute has arisen, showing again how closely linked the Tyroleans are to Italy. This time it is over the discovery of a 4,000-year-old corpse in a melting glacier. The Italian authorities claim that when the body was discovered, there was a fog that prevented them from realizing that the location of the discovery was actually on the Italian and not the Austrian part of the glacier!

AUSTRIA'S OLDEST RESIDENT

At the end of 1990 the son of a mountain guide was startled to discover the body of a man under the melting ice of a glacier in the south of Tyrol. Usually such bodies are victims of avalanches which happened up to 50 years earlier. This man, however, was clutching an axe and beside him lay a knife and a flint. People speculated that maybe the body was up to 500 years old, but glacier specialists said it was unlikely that a glacier could preserve a body for that length of time. This body was remarkably well preserved—the skin could still be seen and muscle tissue remained. The skeleton was complete and showed signs of violent injuries to the head and back.

The body was brought by helicopter to the University of Innsbruck where, to everyone's surprise, it was determined that it was in fact 4,000 years old. This Bronze Age man was wearing shoes made of hide, lined with hay, and near the body were found pieces of birch bark sewn together and chamois hairs. Also found were a wooden backpack, a stone necklace and a leather pouch containing a flint light. How were this man and his possessions preserved for so long? One suggestion is that he might have been mummified by freezing air before falling into the glacier.

"...the first day was so lovely that I determined to stay for a second, and the second was so lovely that I have decided to stay here for the time being."
— the German composer Johannes Brahms describing an unplanned holiday he spent in Carinthia

A small timber mill in Carinthia.

THE PEOPLE OF CARINTHIA

Like Burgenland, Carinthia is a province with a non-German speaking population. The minority language is Slovene, spoken by the ancestors of Slovenes who settled in the area centuries ago. The Slovenes in Carinthia are proud of their language and are fighting to keep it in use.

At the end of World War I, when a slice of Hungary became Austrian and a part of Tyrol became Italian, something similar was happening in this part of Austria. The result was that Austria had to give slices of Carinthia to the then new nation of Yugoslavia as well as Italy. Today, many visitors to the Slovene capital of Ljubljana in Yugoslavia remark on the Austrian feel of that city.

While Tyrol has its 4,000-year-old Austrian ancestor, Carinthia can boast of its rich Celtic background. At Magdalensberg in Carinthia the largest Celtic settlement in Europe has been excavated and it is an important archeological site.

Nowadays, the people of Carinthia are mostly farmers with small farms or workers in the economically important magnesite mines.

THE PEOPLE OF VORARLBERG

The Austrians of Vorarlberg live as close to Paris as they do to Vienna and this is one way of explaining the fact that the people of this most westerly province have an identity of their own. The German they speak sounds more like Swiss German than the typically Austrian German heard in most other parts of the country, which is not that surprising given that Zurich, the capital of Switzerland, is only an hour's drive away while Vienna would take a day's driving to reach.

Both the Swiss and the people of Vorarlberg are descended from the ancient German Alemannic tribes that dominated this part of Central Europe in the 3rd century B.C. This explains why the people of Vorarlberg have a dialect that is quite distinct from the German spoken in other parts of Austria.

Vorarlberg is the most traditional part of Austria where people still wear their traditional costumes—and not just for a tourist festival. There was a time when each valley community would have proudly displayed its own distinctive costume.

However, the process of modernization is making such distinctions of dress less and less meaningful. Nevertheless, the people of Vorarlberg are proud of their traditions and customs and they still retain an individuality that prevents Austrian culture from being completely homogeneous.

A little Austrian girl all dressed up to go to a wedding.

"Biegen, nicht brechen" (Bend, but do not break)
— The unofficial motto of the city of Vienna

THE VIENNESE

Vienna is not just the capital of Austria but a province in its own right, holding over 20% of the country's population. There is also a significant Czech community numbering over 5,000 and a much larger number of foreign workers, mostly from Yugoslavia.

There is a stereotype of the Viennese citizen: elegant, sophisticated, artistic, a lover of classical music and cream pastries, one who studies newspapers for hours in a coffee house where smart waiters come and go balancing trays filled with glasses of water. As with so many aspects of Austrian culture, the explanation for this lies with history.

The Austrian Empire came to a sudden end after World War I, but imperial attitudes did not die quite so quickly. Vienna, once the capital city of a great empire, has taken on a rich cosmopolitan character. It was the one city most patronized by artists and intellectuals and even ordinary citizens felt a sense of being the aristocrats of Austria.

In the 1990s the remnants of the imperial past can be recognized in the mentality of the Viennese, though a farmer from Vorarlberg might be more quick to dismiss such an attitude as pompous snobbery. In return, when the Viennese refer to Vorarlberg as *Ländle*, meaning "the little province," they are only being semi-affectionate for there is an element of big-city snobbery in their attitude to the agricultural province so far to the west.

The legacy of the past can also be seen in the Viennese telephone directory: foreign-sounding names that are obviously not German crop up regularly. Most families in Vienna probably have a grandmother or great-grandfather of Czech or Hungarian descent and the Viennese are proud of their rich cultural heritage.

A public ballroom concert. A reminder of the charm and elegance of Vienna in the 18th century.

FAMOUS AUSTRIAN ARTISTS AND INTELLECTUALS

SIGMUND FREUD (1856–1939) Freud was born in what is now Czechoslovakia but he spent most of his life in Vienna. He finally left Vienna when the Nazis arrived in 1938 and started sending Jews to prison camps. The Jewish Freud fled to London where he died the following year. Freud is the most famous psychologist of all time; he put forward the now commonly accepted idea of the "unconscious"—powerful feelings and instincts which are not consciously accepted yet which determine our behavior, especially behavior which is considered irrational or odd.

Sigmund Freud

LUDWIG WITTGENSTEIN (1889–1951) Wittgenstein, one of the most important philosophers of the 20th century, was born into a rich and sophisticated Austrian family. His commitment to philosophy was so strong that he had little regard for material possessions and when he inherited a large family fortune he gave it all away. After serving in the Austrian army in World War I he traveled to England where he eventually became a professor of philosophy at Cambridge University, before giving that up too, for the same reason he gave away his family fortune—he found it of no use.

OSKAR KOKOSCHKA (1886–1980) One of the great 20th-century artists, Kokoschka's work is famous for its humanist themes and intense landscapes painted with fluid, thick colors. Kokoschka was educated in Vienna and he returned to the city again and again but his socialist convictions and outspoken criticisms of society earned him the hatred of the Nazis. Although he was not a Jew he fled Vienna, like Freud did in 1938, because he knew he would never survive under their regime.

LIFESTYLE

AUSTRIANS ARE FRIENDLY, courteous people who appreciate the virtues of a civilized existence. They have lived through, or heard about from their parents, the deprivations and turmoil of the Nazi period and have no desire to return to those days. Economic prosperity and low unemployment have provided the basis for a lifestyle that values consensus above conflict. Austrians seek to balance the world of work and thrift with time for conversation and the enjoyment of good food, wine and music.

When guests arrive at an Austrian home for a meal it is customary for the hostess to be presented with a small bunch of flowers. It is a way of saying "thank you" for preparing a meal.

Austria has compulsory military service for males lasting less than a year, but with periods of recall later for retraining. The army is more of a militia when compared to the armies of the United States or Britain and does not see itself becoming involved in military conflicts. Austrians do not see their army as an aggressive force, and when Communism in Europe collapsed in the 1990s there were calls to disband the army altogether.

The implications of the breakup of the USSR and the end of the Cold War would be the kind of topic talked and argued about in two of the most popular locations for socializing in Austria: the coffee house and the wine tavern. Over coffee, wine or water Austrians love to meet and talk and talk...and talk.

Opposite: **The café—a favorite meeting place for Austrians to eat, drink and talk.**

Below: **The wine tavern— another favorite Austrian haunt. It isn't just the wine but also the food and conversation that draw people.**

The Austrian flag. Behind closed doors, union leaders and employers negotiate price and wage agreements.

THE SOCIAL PARTNERSHIP

The Social Partnership is the name given to the voluntary cooperation that exists between employers and employees and it reflects the new attitude to social and economic life that emerged after World War II. Representatives from the trade unions meet behind closed doors with leaders of industry and commerce and they thrash out matters of policy concerning price increases and questions of wages. Such meetings have no legal or constitutional standing but the compromises that are made at these meetings filter through to parliament and influence the decisions made there.

The Social Partnership is characteristic of the Austrian way of doing things. Issues that could lead to confrontation and bitterness are avoided and compromises are seen as the best way of dealing with problems.

FACTS AND FIGURES

Literacy rate: virtually 100%

Hospital beds: 1 per 91 persons

Infant mortality rate: per 1,000 live births—10.3

Military expenditure: 1.3% of GNP (world average is 6%)

Average household size: 2.6 persons

Birth rate: per 1,000 population—11.5; legitimate: 76.7%; illegitimate: 23.3%

Divorce rate: per 1,000 population—1.9

Major causes of death: per 100,000 population—diseases of the circulatory system, including heart disease 617.9; cancer 246.1; diseases of the respiratory system 57.7; accidents 51.4

THE COFFEE HOUSE

The coffee house is not just a place for drinking coffee but is more a way of life for Austrians whose love of coffee dates to the end of the 17th century when the Turks were laying siege to Vienna. When defeat was imminent the Turks retreated in a hurry leaving behind hundreds of sacks filled with coffee beans. Apparently, the Viennese didn't have a clue what the brown beans were and it was left to an Austrian merchant who had traveled to Turkey to realize what could be done with them. He opened the first coffee house and experimented with the beans until he found a taste the citizens couldn't resist.

The Viennese coffee house is now a national institution and during the course of the day a typical cross section of the capital's citizens will make a visit: office workers pop in for breakfast, students stay for hours with their textbooks, business people talk shop, shoppers have a break and, at any time of the day, the newspaper addict will be seen systematically working his way through the racks of national and international papers that are provided for customers to read. After an initial coffee the waiter will bring fresh glasses of water. Regular patrons will have their own table.

A waitress clearing the table. Glasses of water are always brought by a waiter or waitress whenever coffee is ordered.

People enjoying the food in a hotel café in Vienna.

THE HEURIGER

The *Heuriger* is a unique kind of wine tavern found most commonly in Vienna and eastern Austria. The word means "this year's" so, strictly speaking, only new wines are available and this is indicated by a sprig of fir or pine or a wreath of holly being placed over the door of the tavern. Inside the tavern Austrians sit around tables talking about matters crucial and trivial but always with equal animation. Buffet-style hot and cold food will normally be available and in the larger *Heurige* (plural), especially those in tourist areas, live music is played.

A visit to the *Heuriger* is quite unlike a bar or pub in the United States. It is frequently a family occasion with children, even dogs, welcome to come along. The wine can be served mixed with soda water, known as a *Gespritzter*, and with plenty of food available it is not unusual for a group of friends to stay chatting and socializing all evening and night.

There are about 800 families growing wine in the area around Vienna and some 500 or more *Heurige* to pour out the 12 million glasses of wine that Austrians drink every year.

Dairy cows and a timbered home in Salzau.

LIFE IN THE COUNTRYSIDE

A rural family in Tyrol could live in a farmhouse that had belonged to the family for 200 years. The farmhouse itself would be made of stone and wood with a bell tower on top to summon the men from the fields at lunchtime. In the countryside Roman Catholicism is more deeply ingrained in the lifestyle of the people than in the cities.

A typical farm has about 50 acres of woodlands and pasture, half a dozen cows, more calves, a few pigs and definitely a dozen or more hens. In the summer the cows are taken up into the Alpine pastures and brought down again in late autumn. In the past, a harsh Alpine winter was spent repairing tools, living off dried meats and cheeses and engaging in handicrafts and weaving. The animals would be kept indoors and fed hay.

Farmers also act as part-time mountain guides or ski instuctors during the tourist season.

Nowadays, during the winter months, the cattle are still kept indoors but in western Austria especially, tourism offers the possibility of alternative employment and many farmers depend on this to supplement their income. The living room is converted into a bedroom and the kitchen becomes the center of family life for a few months. When the snow melts and the tourists depart, the soil is loosened, potatoes and corn are planted and the cycle begins again.

Cheese is still made on some farms, though it most likely is the grandparents who have this skill. Bread-making is more common and a simple lunch can be made out of *Roggenbrot* (rye bread). A weekly ritual is the trip to church every Sunday and, for the men, a game of *Watten* (a card game) after Mass, over a few mugs of beer in the local pub.

EDUCATION

School is compulsory, with all children attending *Volksschulen* (primary schools) between the ages of six and 10. After the 10th year a "two-track system" enforces a separation, with some 80% of students attending *Hauptschulen* (general secondary schools) and a minority attending the more prestigious *Allgemeinbildende Höhere Schulen* (upper-level secondary schools). All students will have lessons in English as a second language. After primary education it is also possible to pursue vocational training by attending the medium-level or higher-level technical schools. Students attend these schools for careers in industry, agriculture, forestry, nursing, tourism or social work.

From both the upper-level technical schools or the *Allgemeinbildende Höhere Schulen* students can proceed to university, many of which have a long history. The University of Vienna, for example, was founded in 1365 and this makes it the oldest university in German-speaking Europe. Universities in Graz and Innsbruck were founded in the 16th and 17th centuries respectively and Graz and Vienna also boast prestigious technical universities. Criticisms about the elitist character of Austrian universities are unfounded.

Young people in a park in Vienna. There is always time for fun and relaxation after lessons.

There are equal opportunities for all Austrians to receive an education; even the children of foreign workers in Austria have the same right to free education as the Austrian child (i.e., no school fees, free transportation to and from school and free textbooks). In 1986 as many as 18.5% of all pupils of compulsory school age in Vienna were the children of foreign workers.

A street musician in jester's garb. If this is interpreted as self-employment, this street musician may be entitled to social insurance protection. However, sociologists call this form of "employment" a sort of disguised begging.

SOCIAL SECURITY

Austria has one of the best social welfare systems in the world. Compulsory national health insurance covers the medical expenses of visits to the doctor or stays in the hospital. Similarly, workers are protected against financial loss in the event of sickness or accident. Social insurance protection has also been extended to self-employed people, like farmers and independent business people. Unemployment benefits average out at nearly half the previous normal earnings, although such benefits are not paid out indefinitely. Even in the case of death, the benefits include a contribution to funeral expenses.

There are 13 legal holidays annually and Austrian workers receive five weeks of paid vacation every year. After retirement (65 for men and 60 for women), old-age pensions are paid and disability pensions are paid regardless of age.

All these benefits are financed by a combination of employers' and employees' contributions plus government funds.

With more than a quarter of the proceeds of its economic growth being channeled into the area of social security, Austria can justly claim to be one of the most advanced of all welfare states. Inevitably, there is the possibility of the system being exploited by those who really could look after themselves financially. Stories of social security "scroungers" are often heard at the *Heuriger* but even so, Austria can be proud of its social welfare system.

Old people's home in Salzburg. The elderly are very well taken care of under Austria's excellent social welfare system.

THE AUSTRIAN LIFE CYCLE

In a country where 84% of the people call themselves Roman Catholics, it is not surprising that baptism functions as one of the earliest rites of passage. Parents, together with relatives and friends, bring their young baby along to the church where the priest performs a simple ceremony that initiates the baby into the Roman Catholic Church.

Marriage, for practicing Roman Catholics, must be a church affair. After the wedding the couple will go off for their honeymoon and, if they can afford it, this will often mean a visit to another European country.

A graveyard—90% of Austrian funerals are held in a church.

Funerals are also church affairs, beginning with a ceremony in the church and then continued at the graveyard as the coffin is lowered into the ground. Before the funeral the body will be laid out at rest for family and friends to pay their respects.

In the countryside traditional customs and celebrations have survived and there are various rites that have their origins in the passing of the seasons. The end of winter and the advent of spring are marked by carnivals and processions and later in the year, during the fall, there are thanksgiving ceremonies and country fairs. Some of the parades that are still observed today have their origins in pre-Christian times.

In a "ghosts' parade" costumed men wearing large wooden masks move through the streets in an eerie procession—a throwback to the days of pagan spirit worship.

TRADITIONAL DRESS

The most characteristic Austrian traditional dress for women is the *Dirndl,* which consists of an embroidered blouse with a laced-up bodice worn over a full skirt and apron. Men wear *Lederhosen* (leather shorts) with ornamental suspenders and belts. Jackets are short without lapels. Distinctive hats are worn.

Today these clothes are mainly worn for festive or tourist occasions. Their authenticity, though, is kept alive by the strict regional differences that demarcate the individual items of dress. The style of the hats, for example, varies not just from one region to another but even from one valley to another.

Headgear for women is sometimes very distinctively braided with gold. A woman's hat from Vorarlberg, instead of resting on the head, rises from it looking as though it has been put on upside down. Traditional costumes from the Salzkammergut area in central Austria resemble the dress of 18th-century gentlemen and ladies, with the gentlemen donning long jackets and white socks pulled up to the knee and tied with a colored ribbon.

Almabtrieb is a festival where the cows are "thanked" and brought down from the mountain pastures. People wear traditional dress for this festival.

RELIGION

AT THE LAST CENSUS, 84% of Austrians declared themselves Roman Catholic, 6% Protestant, 4% from other creeds and 6% as having no religion. Until the fall of the Hapsburg Empire the Church and the state were one, but now they are separated, so divorce and abortion are legally possible even though the Church does not allow it. It is also the case that Roman Catholicism is more widely practiced in the countryside than in the cities, where people may profess themselves Roman Catholic, but do not necessarily observe it in their daily lives. Whether practiced or not, Austria's adherence to Roman Catholicism is one factor that distinguishes its people from those in the neighboring countries. And while churchgoing is on the decrease, 70% of the population still have a church wedding, 90% have their children baptized and 90% are given a church funeral ceremony.

Opposite: **St. Stephen's Cathedral with its high steeple is the focal point of Vienna. The old wood work of the roof was burned in the last days of World War II, but has since been completely rebuilt in steel.**

Below: **Candles are lit by devout worshipers inside St. Stephen's Cathedral.**

Catacomb in the rock, St. Peter's Cemetery in Salzburg. In Austrian churches, carvings which depict episodes in the life of Christ are placed around the inside perimeter of the church. At designated times of the week, devotees will stop and pray at each tableau.

ROMAN CATHOLICISM

The beginning of Roman Catholicism in Austria lies with the missionaries who founded monasteries as far back as A.D. 700. Salzburg, for example, became the center of a monastic school, where manuscripts were copied with a religious zeal that seems like artistic inspiration. The manuscripts that survived, and the interlacing patterns found in the few extant carvings, bear a close resemblance to the Irish designs of the Book of Kells.

Due to the rich musical tradition in Austria the Sunday Mass is often accompanied by choirs and organ music. The great Austrian musicians—Mozart and Schubert—wrote entire compositions to accompany the Roman Catholic Mass, "operas for the angels" as Mozart called his.

MONASTERIES

The Cistercians have always been famous for their strict austerity. During the great spread of monastic houses in the 11th and 12th centuries they moved into Austria where they settled on formerly unproductive land and worked extremely hard as agriculturalists. In time they grew wealthy and two branches formed, the Trappists, who continued to follow the original rules, and another branch with fewer restrictions. Because Austria remained Roman Catholic the monks didn't suffer as badly during the Protestant Reformation as their counterparts did in other parts of Europe, when Roman Catholic churches and monasteries were under attack.

Today in Austria Cistercian monasteries that were founded in the 12th century continue to exist and function. The monks wear the same garb: black scapula, white cassock with a dark collar. Many of the abbeys have survived by converting part of their buildings into private schools or by leasing out their extensive farmland.

RELIGIOUS FESTIVALS

The Crucifix, depicting the crucifixion of Christ for the sins of the world. Such wayside shrines are found all over the countryside.

Corpus Christi, May 30 each year, is a religious holiday celebrated throughout the country. Colorful processions and parades take place in towns and villages across Austria and in some places it provides an occasion for traditional costumes to be worn.

All Souls' Day is another event in the religious calendar when small villages will come alive with a procession led by the village band with tall white feathers in their caps. The priest will often have a loudspeaker to lead the prayers and chants of the villagers as they walk to the village cemetery. Here candles flicker by the graves that are surrounded by flowers placed there by the relatives of the dead. It is a day for commemorating the faithful departed, baptized Roman Catholics who are believed to be in purgatory because they have died with guilt of lesser sins on their souls. Roman Catholics believe that the prayers of the faithful still on earth will help cleanse the souls of these departed.

On Good Friday, a service with Holy Communion is held in remembrance of the death of Jesus Christ on the cross for the sins of the world. Three days later, on Easter Sunday, the Resurrection of Christ is celebrated.

The day before Christmas is celebrated throughout Austria with midnight Masses. *Silent Night, Holy Night*, heard throughout the Christian world at this time of year, was written by an Austrian, Franz Gruber. It was first performed on Christmas Eve in 1818 in a church in the village of Oberndorf. The carol was accompanied by the guitar because, as the story goes, mice had gnawed the organ's bellows. All over the country, churches will be crowded with people attending midnight Mass, especially St. Stephen's Cathedral in Vienna where entrance tickets are distributed long before December 25.

A chapel in winter at Christmas time. The birth of Jesus Christ is celebrated throughout Austria.

AUSTRIAN SAINTS

St. Martin's Day on November 11 is not officially a public holiday but it comes very close to being one. Restaurants traditionally serve roast goose and red cabbage in honor of the patron saint of owners of bars and innkeepers. In Burgenland, *Martinigansl* (Martin's goose), or *Ganslessen* (goose eating) as it is also called, is a big event because St. Martin is the patron saint of that province and parades and ceremonies take place as a matter of course.

Florian was a man who during the 4th century chose to drown himself rather than submit to the worship of the pagan Roman gods. On the site of his tomb the Augustinian monks built a monastery that is still standing. The town itself that grew up around it is called St. Florian.

OTHER RELIGIONS

Austrian Protestants have been allowed to practice their religion since 1791 and when Burgenland was transferred from Hungary to Austria in 1921 this significantly increased the number of Protestants in the country as a whole.

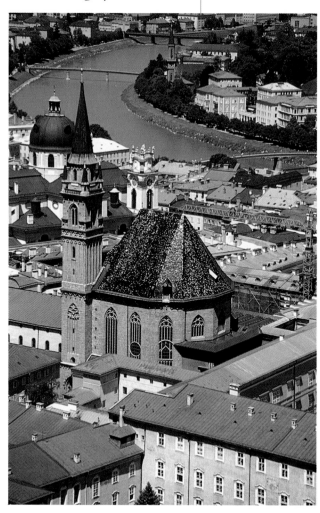

Vienna is less religiously homogenous than any other part of Austria. Therefore, the presence of other religions can be seen in Vienna. The Jews, for example, can trace their existence in Austria back to the 9th century. They played a vitally important part in the cultural life of the capital especially at the turn of the century.

After World War II there were only 2,000 of the 190,000 Jews left in Vienna as a result of the "final solution" of the Nazis. Nowadays there are about 10,000 Jews in Vienna and very few anywhere else in Austria.

Islam also has a presence in Vienna mainly due to the influx of foreign workers from Moslem Turkey and certain parts of Yugoslavia. In 1978 the Islamic Center was completed, providing a mosque as well as cultural and social services.

LANGUAGE

AUSTRIA IS THE ONLY COUNTRY, apart from Germany of course, where German is the national language. German is one of the main languages of the Western world, spoken by over 100 million people. It is one of the four languages spoken in Switzerland. German is also used in parts of eastern France and Belgium and northern Italy. In the United States, over 6 million people speak German and there are communities of German-speaking people spread across the world from the USSR to Latin America.

Austrian German does not sound the same as the German spoken in Germany. Within a few moments it is possible to recognize an Austrian from a German by the pronunciation of the language.

A broad division can be made between High German and Low German. These are two dialects that have their origins in the south and north of Germany respectively. However, High German has become the standard written language and is used as the language for official communication. In Austria there is an equivalent High Austrian German, which is the "official" formal German used.

Opposite: **A poster column in downtown Vienna. For official matters a formal German language is used.**

Below: **A wrought iron sign in German. The national language of Austria is German.**

AUSTRIAN GERMAN

Not only is the German spoken in Austria different from the German of Germany but the German spoken in one part of Austria is different from that of another region. The dialects of Austria are more distinct than those of Germany and a dialect speaker from Vorarlberg, for instance, could have some difficulty conversing with a local speaker from eastern Austria. In the mountainous areas of west Austria it is often the case that the inhabitants of one valley will have a quite separate dialect from those living in a neighboring valley which could only be a few miles away.

A welcome sign in Styria. Austrians are warm and courteous in both behavior and speech.

In Vorarlberg the German spoken is very similar to the German heard in neighboring Switzerland and this can be traced back to their common roots with the Alemannic tribes that occupied this part of Central Europe in the 7th century. In Vienna on the other hand the city's dialect, known as *Wienerisch*, has developed its own unique identity. A native of Tyrol would recognize the *Wienerisch* as quickly as a Californian would recognize a southern drawl. The ending "erl" is tacked onto nouns turning them into diminutives. For example, the word for "kiss" in High German is *Kuss* but in *Wienerisch*, it becomes *Busserl*.

More generally, Austrian German is more melodious and softer than the German of Germany. For example, a German will say *guten Morgen* (good morning) with a pronounced stress on certain syllables ("GOO-ten MOR-gen") whereas an Austrian will allow the sounds to flow more easily into one another and the sharpness will be softened ("gooten-mOrgen").

THE LANGUAGE OF COURTESY

In the imperial past there were strict codes of formal behavior that governed one's social behavior. This may have been due to the ethnic melting pot of the Hapsburg Empire and the consequent need for a common language.

The legacy is a certain formality in the Austrian way of doing things and this is mirrored in the language. There are courteous forms of address that strike the outsider as odd, quaint or just ridiculous. A doctor, for instance, is typically referred to as *Herr Doktor*, a town councilor will be a *Herr Geheimrat* and a lady will be referred to as *gnädige Frau*.

Such formality is only an outward show and behind it there is a cheerful spirit of friendliness. An often repeated saying is that in Berlin they will tell you that the situation is serious but not desperate; in Vienna they will tell you that it is desperate but not serious.

Two men in friendly conversation. The formal and polite forms of addressing people used in the imperial past are still in active use today.

GERMAN PRONUNCIATION

For a long time German was written in a Gothic style known as *Fraktur,* dating back to the 14th century, but this has now been replaced by standardized Roman characters which make the task of pronunciation a lot easier.

SOUND/LETTER	PRONUNCIATION
j	*y*—e.g. *ja* (yes) is pronounced "ya"
w	*v*—e.g. Raymond Weil is pronounced Raymond "Veil"
v	*f*—e.g. *vier* (four) is pronounced "fier"

Diphthongs are gliding speech sounds made by pronouncing two vowels or consonants quickly one after another.

sch	*sh*—e.g. *Schnee* (snow)
st	*sht*—e.g. *Strasse* (street)
sp	*shp*—e.g. *sprechen* (to speak)

LONG GERMAN WORDS

In an essay written by Mark Twain, he commented on the ability of the German language to join words together to form new words. This ease of forming compounds does sometimes result in very long words. These long words themselves can easily be split up into their different components and the meaning is always very clear. For example, the word *Volksschullehrerseminar* is made up of four separate words:

Volks (people or public)

Schul (school)

Lehrer (teacher)

Seminar (seminary)

So the word means a "public-school-teachers-seminary," or, in more normal English, a "training college for elementary-school teachers."

Sometimes, though, the compounding can stretch anyone's linguistic ability. Here is the special German title for the captain of a steamboat on the Danube river: *Donaudampfschiffahrtsgesellschaftkapitän*.

A horse and carriage sign in a town in Styria. In a country where some words are so long that they can hardly be pronounced, there is room for some things where words are not needed.

"The rights of minorities to have their own organizations and meetings, and to have newspapers, etc. in their own language; their right to elementary education in their own language; in administrative districts with a mixed-language population, the admission of Crotian and Slovenian as an official language, and the provision of bilingual signs to indicate place-names, etc."

—Provisions of Article 7 of the Constitution

ENGLISH AND GERMAN

Early in the Christian era the numerous Germanic tribes migrated on a large scale and some ended up in Britain where they had a decisive influence on the English language. In fact, English is a Germanic language and there are many similarities between the two vocabularies. The following words are spelled the same in both languages and mean exactly the same:

blind
Finger
Ring
Butter
Hand
warm

The reason why some of the words in the above list begin with a capital letter and some don't is that German is the only language where all nouns begin with a capital letter.

Other words are so similar that the link between the two languages is clear:

Vater (but pronounced "fahter") and father
Mutter and mother
Fisch and fish
gut and good
Buch and book
Gott and God
Freund and friend

More recently the following German words have entered the English language:

kindergarten (a nursery school)
lager (a light beer)
poodle (a small dog with thick curly hair)
hinterland (the inner part of a country beyond the coast)
blitzkrieg (a sudden heavy attack, abbreviated to blitz)

Even the word "hamburger," which seems so American, is named after the German city of Hamburg.

MINORITY LANGUAGES

In Burgenland the Croatian minority are concerned about the possible decline of their language and culture and one bone of contention has been the provision of bilingual place-names. According to the Austrian constitution the rights of the Slovene and Croatian minorities are guaranteed and although an Ethnic Groups Act was passed in 1976 it is still the case that bilingual place-names are dependent upon one-quarter of the population in a given area belonging to a minority group. This effectively works against the Croat language and the issue remains unresolved, causing a certain amount of unhappiness and disappointment.

In Carinthia the minority language is Slovene, spoken by the ancestors of the Slovenes who settled in the area centuries ago. As with Burgenland's minority Croats, the Slovenes of Carinthia, who make up 4% of the province's population, are fighting to keep the non-German names of their villages.

Street signs pointing in all directions. In some regions, minority groups are campaigning for certain places to retain their ethnic, non-German names.

ARTS

THE GREATEST AGE for the arts was the 18th century when music, architecture and painting flourished partly due to the number of patrons that eagerly sought to commission new works and buildings as a way of celebrating their own significance.

It was not just the Hapsburgs who became patrons but the Church also played a significant role, commissioning music for the Mass and artists to design and decorate their churches. Yet the Church and the nobility treated Mozart, their greatest asset, the most shabbily of all, reducing him to debt and poverty and helping to cause his premature death at the age of only 35. Gustav Mahler also suffered abuse from the anti-Semitic press when he was the director of the Vienna Opera.

Opposite: **A street musical puppet show—music plays a large part in the everyday lives of Austrians.**

Below: **The dome of the Salzburg Cathedral. The Church played a big part in promoting the arts in the 18th century.**

The musical and artistic heritage of Austria does not owe everything to the aristocratic patrons of the Church and state. Music is in the blood of Austrians and during the 19th century it would have been uncommon to find a middle-class Viennese family that couldn't put together its own string quartet.

MUSICAL AND ARTISTIC HERITAGE

The people of Austria exhibit their artistic nature in everything they do. Their wood-carvings, wrought iron work, glassware, lace and embroidery show that they have an eye for intricate patterns and elaborate designs. The pursuit of beautiful and fine workmanship can be seen in the detailed nature of their work.

Vienna is synonymous with the art of music and any roll call of the world's greatest composers will include more musicians from Vienna than any other city. Haydn, Johann Strauss and son, Mozart, Schubert and Schönberg were all Austrians. The music of Vienna had a decisive effect on the form of the symphony and the string quartet and the city became the center for new symphonic writing. Beethoven settled there to work as a composer and so did Brahms. Mahler and Richard Strauss, though not Austrian by birth, are considered part of the country's musical life.

Music continues to play an important role in the lives of Austrians, from the folk dances of Tyrol to the studied elegance of performances by the Vienna Philharmonic Orchestra and the Vienna State Opera. Tickets to the Opera House, and those of the Vienna Boys' Choir, are sold out months in advance and dedicated fans make their reservations a year in advance.

Tree carvings in St. Wolfgang. The Austrians display their artistic skill in these tree carvings.

FRANZ JOSEPH HAYDN (1732–1809)

Haydn spent his life in Burgenland under the patronage of two wealthy Hungarian princes and he lived in relative comfort and ease. In his time he became the idol of the European intelligentsia and, with the permission of his patron, made two famous trips to London and Ireland. He lived happily with the knowledge that "...I have had the good fortune to please almost everywhere..."

Haydn was interested in the structure of music and he is credited with developing the symphony into its present form.

He used folk dance music in his compositions and his *Emperor* string quartet, which was composed for the Austrian national anthem during the monarchy, has its musical origins in a foot-stomping dance for farmers. The dance rhythms are recognizable at the beginning and end of the piece. He also used the rustic country waltz *Landler* in his symphonies and in the oratorio *The Creation*.

FRANZ SCHUBERT (1797–1828)

Schubert was born in Vienna, and except for brief excursions to the country never left the city. As a choir boy in the choir of the Imperial Court Chapel, he received one of the best educations available then in Vienna. He was dismissed from the choir in 1813 when his voice changed. He was too short to join the military service, and so became a school teacher like his father.

Schubert composed songs, operettas and choral pieces. He also wrote symphonies as well as dance pieces for piano, piano sonatas and chamber music. Some of his most well-known songs include *The Trout* and *The Erlking*—the tragic ride of a father trying to outdistance the Erlking, Death.

He was a great admirer of Beethoven and when Schubert died in November 1828, he was buried close to Beethoven. The remains of the two composers were reburied side by side in 1863. Ignored by the newspapers in Vienna when he was alive, the papers printed memorial poems about Schubert when he died. Often dismissed as only a song writer, he was really very versatile as his symphonies, sonatas and quartets have shown.

WOLFGANG AMADEUS MOZART (1756–1791)

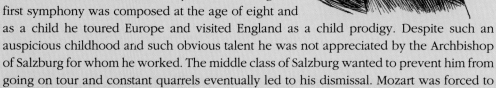

Mozart was born in Salzburg, as any visitor to the city cannot fail to notice, but during his lifetime his genius was not appreciated by the people who lived there. When he died in poverty his wife was not even given the money to pay for his funeral and he was buried in a pauper's grave whose exact location remains unknown. There is no certainty that the skull preserved in the Mozarteum in Salzburg is really his.

Mozart excelled in every musical medium of his time and is the most universal composer in Western history. At the age of three he was playing the harpsichord and he took to the violin without any formal training. His first symphony was composed at the age of eight and as a child he toured Europe and visited England as a child prodigy. Despite such an auspicious childhood and such obvious talent he was not appreciated by the Archbishop of Salzburg for whom he worked. The middle class of Salzburg wanted to prevent him from going on tour and constant quarrels eventually led to his dismissal. Mozart was forced to

scratch out a living by traveling across Europe looking for work. At one stage he was appointed the Imperial and Royal Chamber Composer for the Hapsburg emperor Joseph II, but the grand title meant little for he was badly underpaid and soon found himself in debt.

The constant traveling took a toll on his health and he died in 1791 in Salzburg, singing strains from his last work, the *Requiem*. At the age of 35 he had composed 50 symphonies, 22 operas and innumerable other works. Some 30 years ago, 24 piano sonatas of his were discovered in the attic of a house in Vienna. Mozart's compositions are often identified by the letter "K." followed by a number. This "K." stands for Ludwig von Köchel, who cataloged Mozart's compositions into chronological order.

Mozart was not recognized for his greatness during his short life but his musical genius has been acclaimed all over the world after his death. For the first 100 years after his death, Mozart's name did not fade into oblivion but was kept alive because performances of his music were still being given to live audiences. With modern technology—such as radios, records, cassette tapes, compact discs and video tapes— Mozart's music has reached the far corners of the world and gained popularity in different cultures of the world, many of which Mozart himself would not even have known existed.

Although the music of Mozart is best known for its gaiety and liveliness it also possesses a melancholic strain and reflects the spirit of the Enlightenment. His opera *The Marriage of Figaro* tells the tale of a struggle between a servant and a master and celebrates the dignity of the common man. Mozart himself angered the Archbishop by declaring that he, the musician, "probably had more nobility than a count."

In 1991, music centers from all over the world held performances of Mozart's work to commemorate the 200th anniversary of his death, from symphonic and chamber music to operas, sacred works and solo keyboard pieces.

In New York's Lincoln Center for example, all the city's 11 arts organizations combined their efforts to perform the entire catalog of Mozart's music. Lectures and exhibitions were also organized for school children—recognition surely, for a true musical genius.

STRAUSS, JOHANN, SR. (1804–1849) AND JOHANN, JR. (1825–1899)

Like the Hapsburg royal family who ruled the empire, the pair of father and son were the kings of Vienna's social dance life in the 1800s. Their music entertained at the cafés and outdoor gardens while customers (including other composers) had their coffee, beer and sausages.

Johann Sr. ran away from being a bookbinder's apprentice to study the violin and a bit of music theory. In his mid-20s he formed his own group and as his reputation spread, his orchestra became the official dance orchestra for Vienna court balls. His compositions include more than 150 waltzes as well as music for other dance forms of the day.

Johann Jr. (whose statue is shown above) immortalized Vienna with his famous *Blue Danube Waltz*. When his father died in 1849, he took over the orchestra and gained even greater popularity than his father. He toured as far as the United States and Russia. He also wrote operettas in addition to waltzes and dance music. When he died, the whole era of "Dancing Vienna" also came to an end.

THE WALTZ

The waltz, known as the *Landler* before being christened the waltz, has its origin in Austria as a traditional dance in which partners came together in each other's arms and then turned with a hop and a step. It gained the interest of the upper classes but because they were always dressed in their fashionable costumes for appearances at court, the dance was gradually modified to suit the fact that their elegant dress was not comfortable or versatile enough to allow them to move so quickly. Also, the smooth ballroom floors were different from the stone floors where the dance originated and this too encouraged a slower movement.

What remained, though, was the close physical contact and, as the popular Viennese dance became the vogue in fashionable circles across Europe, it provoked critics. In 1818, the *Times* newspaper of London labeled it "that indecent foreign dance" and called on every conscientious parent to be aware of the moral danger of "so fatal a contagion." But at the time the partners in a waltz didn't actually come together that closely! It wasn't until the end of the 19th century that waltzers actually moved together in the close embrace that now characterizes the dance.

Waltzers in a public ballroom. In the 19th century, such dancing was labeled as indecent.

The most enduring and famous waltz music was composed by Johann Strauss Sr. in the first half of the 19th century, and then later by his son Johann Strauss Jr. who extended the range of the waltz so that the music became orchestral in character.

93

The Tyrol Opera House—music is not confined only to Salzburg and Vienna. Concerts and operas are performed all over Austria.

Arnold Schönberg

20TH-CENTURY MUSIC

Austria's amazing musical talent did not end with Mozart, Haydn and Strauss. In fact the most revolutionary composer of the 20th century is also Austrian: Arnold Schönberg (1874–1951). He began as a self-taught composer and went on to produce the single most important innovation in post-classical music. With his *Three Piano Pieces* op. 11 of 1909, he created a new dimension of tonality, a method of composing using 12 interrelated notes. The composer chooses any 12 consecutive tones, or notes, but uses them in any order as long as they are all used before repeating one. Conventional harmony is abandoned though his works demonstrate an understanding of classical notions of form and technique.

In a lighter vein the 20th century also saw the emergence of Franz Lehár, known as the uncrowned king of the musical-comedy stage. His operetta *Die lustige Witwe* (*The Merry Widow*) has been translated into 90 languages.

Austria's rich musical heritage should continue to flourish. Music is a compulsory subject in elementary and secondary schools and even for 15- to 18-year-olds there are two hours of music each week, which can only be replaced by art during their last two years in school. A large proportion of children are enrolled in private music schools learning an instrument and advanced classes are taught at the various private conservatories which are situated in the provincial capitals. The most advanced training is available at the three music academies in Vienna, Salzburg and Graz. These are public institutions organized like universities, but quite independent of them. At the academies in Vienna and Salzburg up to as many as 50% of the students can be foreigners, especially Americans.

The Austrians' love of music is best seen in the church choirs which continue to sing the great Masses in Latin by Haydn and Mozart. In rural areas amateur ensembles are common, especially brass ensembles playing folk music. At one count there were over 2,000 brass bands with more than 60,000 members, a third of whom were less than 18 years old.

A brass band entertains in a park.

Interior of St. Stephen's Cathedral—high arches and stained glass—a combination of spiritual devotion and artistic skill.

CHURCH ART AND ARCHITECTURE

The rich development of architecture in Austria owes a lot to the monks who founded monasteries and abbeys and were rich enough to commission large-scale buildings. At first the Romanesque style was used, following Roman models of building with rounded arches and vaults with massive walls to carry their weight.

With the development of the Gothic style in Europe, architects extended the height of the buildings by using pointed arches and stone ribs to form the vaults. Outside walls helped take the downward thrust of these high arches. Projecting from these outside walls, curved bridges connected to the arches and designed to take the lateral thrust of these arches extended (or "flew") to the ground—hence the term "flying buttresses." The resulting interiors had a sense of spaciousness. There was more room for windows which encouraged the making of stained glass.

As the vaults grew higher the art work became more and more ornate and ornamental. Doorways were carved and sculptures were added, first in wood and later in stone. St. Stephen's Cathedral in Vienna, which had its own workshop for sculptors, started out as a Romanesque building and was later converted to the Gothic style. Before it was rebuilt as a result of war damage in 1945, it had 30,000 wooden beams supporting the roof.

The Church was not just the focus of attention for architects and sculptors. At a time when religion dominated so many forms of artistic expression, painters were commissioned to paint the elaborately carved altars.

In the 17th century the Baroque style of architecture developed from the Gothic. There are many examples of this exuberant and spectacular style in Austria. The best example is the abbey at Melk, originally a Benedictine abbey but rebuilt in the Baroque style in the 18th century.

The center of Vienna is an architectural treat all by itself. The Ringstrasse, the ring road that encircles the city center, is the site of various important buildings, each built in a different style toward the end of the 19th century. The parliament building resembles a Greek temple whereas the university imitates the style of an Italian Renaissance palace. The city hall is more Gothic and Flemish in character. The most impressive looking of all is the State Opera House. It attracted such severe criticism when it was built, that one of the architects committed suicide as a result.

A mural on the entrance to a small church. The mural depicts scenes of Jesus Christ's ordeal going up Mount Calvary.

Right: **Belvedere Palace was built for Prince Eugene as a summer residence after he successfully protected the empire from Turkish invaders.**

Below: **Furnace in the Imperial Palace, Vienna. Austrian interest in art and good living is shown in the opulence of Empress Maria Theresa's time.**

A special architectural wonder found in Austria is the castles and stately homes built for the aristocrats during the years of the Hapsburgs. A *Schloss* is the residence of nobility and a *Lustschloss* is the aristocrat's summer or winter holiday home. What was once a hunting castle, a *Jagdschloss*, is now the most medieval-looking of all, with wooded beams everywhere, four poster beds, suits of armor propped up in corners and antlers on the walls.

Many of these residences and lodges have been converted into hotels. A few others, such as the hunting lodge at Mayerling, have been replaced by chapels. The many wonderful palaces in Vienna have become famous museums and within their gilded and ornate rococo walls, the splendor and richness of Austria's past have been preserved.

THE VIENNA STATE OPERA

The Vienna State Opera is a state-run institution which requires substantial subsidies each year in order to balance its books. However, this has never caused concern because the majority of Austrians, even if they never make a visit themselves, recognize the State Opera as their country's cultural showcase. The Opera House can stage over 40 different operas during one season, each in its original language, and the standard is probably the highest in the world.

The Vienna Opera House is built like a cake on a platter. It is one of the most resplendent opera houses in the world. In spite of its grandeur, there is provision for the opera fan on a shoe-string budget—standing room tickets are available and "standees" line up on a graded floor with railings in front on which they can lean.

HERBERT VON KARAJAN

Born in 1908 and only recently deceased in July 1989, Herbert von Karajan was one of the world's foremost conductors. A former director of the Vienna State Opera, Karajan's baton-wielding pose has appeared on millions of record and compact disc covers. Karajan, who was born in Salzburg, also founded the city's Easter Festival of music.

THE VIENNA PHILHARMONIC ORCHESTRA

The Vienna Philharmonic Orchestra was founded in 1842 on March 28. On that day, the Orchestra Personnel of the Imperial Court Opera Theater gave their first symphonic concert under the direction of the opera conductor Otto Nicolai. The orchestra honors its founder every year with a "Nicolai Concert."

A visit to the Vienna Philharmonic Orchestra is a very special occasion. Subscribers are part of the capital's cultural aristocracy and tickets are simply not available at the box office. According to tradition, the repertoire is strictly limited to works of the Classic and Romantic periods.

The regular Philharmonic Subscription Concerts as they are known today were introduced in 1860 when the orchestra was directed by Otto Dessoff. In 1870, the orchestra made its permanent home in the main hall of the new concert building of the *Gesellschaft der Musikfreunde*, known better as the *Musikverein*.

The New Year's Day Concert in Vienna is performed by the Vienna Philharmonic Orchestra in this concert hall every year. The program always includes *The Blue Danube Waltz* and *The Radetzky March*. A tradition of the New Year's Day Concert is that *The Radetzky March* is always accompanied by the audience clapping in time with the music. This concert is so famous now that it is transmitted live, through radio and television, to broadcasting stations all over the world. Depending on the program, the Vienna Boys' Choir also performs during the New Year's Day Concert together with the orchestra.

THE VIENNA BOYS' CHOIR

The *Wiener Sängerknaben*, the Vienna Boys' Choir, has been singing morning Mass in the Hofburg Chapel for 500 years. The Hofburg was the official residence of the Hapsburgs. Their numerous recordings and international tours have turned them into another of Austria's musical institutions. New recruits are issued with sailor suits, a dress that helps identify them as the cultural ambassadors they have become when they travel abroad or appear on television. All the boys are aged between eight and 13 and in the chapel they are more often heard than seen from their perch in the high gallery. It is said that in Vienna, it is the secret dream of nearly every boy to be a member of the choir. However, the standards are very high and not everyone who tries for it is selected. Although the maximum age is 13, once the voice of a choir boy changes even before he is 13 years old, he will have to leave.

LITERATURE

Some great European writers were not Austrian by birth but they grew up under the Austrian Empire and it formed the language and content of their writing. One of the most significant of these writers is Franz Kafka, more properly a Czechoslovakian but writing in German. In *The Trial*, he wrote about the Austrian regime as a bureaucratic police state. Rainer Rilke, the poet, has had more influence than any other writer working under the Austrian Empire and his poetry, along with Kafka's novels and short stories, is probably the most anti-bourgeois works of art ever associated with Austria.

Stefan Zweig was born in Austria and his work, like that of Franz Kafka and Rilke, undermines the safe materialism of the Viennese lifestyle. He was very much influenced by the writings of the Viennese psychoanalyst Sigmund Freud. He emigrated to South America and ended his own life there, feeling that the Nazification of Europe offered him no home. Contemporary literature in Austria is considered unexciting and lacking in refinement. The only sparks of controversy have been created by Peter Handke, whose work has received international attention. A drama version of his *Wunschloses Unglück* was produced in New York under the title *A Sorrow Beyond Dreams*. He defined his work by the formula *"Das Fette, an dem ich würge: Österreich"*—"The fat mass I choke on is Austria."

National Theater, Vienna, one of the many theaters where classic and contemporary dramatic works, operettas and comic operas are performed.

LEISURE

AUSTRIANS TAKE LEISURE very seriously. The national sport and leisure activity is skiing and this is so popular that a public opinion poll once suggested that a majority of Austrians ranked the current champion skier as more of a national hero than Wolfgang Amadeus Mozart. When not participating, Austrians are avid spectators of the sport, with ski races held regularly on the glaciers of the Grossglockner and slopes around Innsbruck and other centers. Apart from skiing, playing and watching soccer are also very popular and the Austrian national team is always an able contender for the World Cup.

During the summer, hiking is popular and with 35,000 miles of mountain paths, there is room for everyone. Austria is now considered to have the largest unspoiled landscape in Western Europe and this has a lot to do with the interest in walking. There are routes that traverse the country including ones across snow-clad hills and mountains where avalanches take their annual toll.

Opposite: **Vienna "*Prater*," the Vienna Amusement Park—the giant ferris wheel can be seen from far away. It was built by an English engineer, Walter B. Basset, in 1896. He also built other giant wheels in Chicago, London, Blackpool and Paris but only the Viennese wheel survived. In 1945, the whole thing was destroyed by bombs and fire but was rebuilt, as was the city, in 1946. The ferris wheel has been in constant action since then.**

Below: **Ice rink in Bad Hofgastein—skating is one of the many leisure activities that Austrians enjoy in winter.**

Olympic flames in Innsbruck. The city of Innsbruck in Tyrol has been chosen twice as the center for the Winter Olympic Games.

SKIING

Austrians are introduced to skiing as early as age three so it is not surprising that it is the favorite sport of 68% of all Austrians. A school trip will almost certainly take in a skiing holiday sometime, either during the main season between November and April, or outside the season at one of the year-round resorts above 11,000 feet. All the centers have professional instructors catering to all levels, from absolute beginners to experts.

Of the 50 Olympic gold medals won by Austria, over half are for skiing and the champions who win these medals and other titles become household names. Switzerland is the only country that comes close to Austria in the number of Alpine world championship medals garnered: 140 to Austria's 160. Skiing is more than just a sport; it's an industry. Austria's ski manufacturing industry is the largest in the world with exports accounting for the bulk of sales.

For a long time downhill skiing has been the most popular form but now cross-country skiing (*Langlauf*) is becoming more appealing. Many of the downhill slopes are getting crowded and cross-country skiing takes one away from the crowds. It is also safer and less expensive. There are no great technical hurdles to be overcome and the beginner is spared the indignity of making himself or herself look silly by frequently falling over in the snow. The valley resorts now have prepared cross-country trails with loops and direct routes from one point to another.

Ski tourists like Austria, finding it less impersonal than many of the resorts in Switzerland and Germany. The Austrian art of *Gemütlichkeit* (an attitude which creates a certain kind of leisurely, warm and friendly atmosphere, full of cosiness, geniality and joviality) is appreciated. Austrians and tourists are also drawn to the varied activities available in the bigger ski resorts such as sleigh rides, tobogganing, even yodeling.

A seven-year-old girl tries out her skis in Kirchdorf.

Right: **Hiking is popular everywhere—in towns and in the mountains.**

Below: **The presence of hot springs has made thermal baths in Bad Hofgastein a hot favorite in winter.**

NOT ONLY SKIING

The Alpine terrain of Austria has given rise to other pursuits besides skiing and mountaineering. Hang gliding, ballooning and parapente (a kind of steerable parachute) have been introduced to many of the resorts in recent years. Most Austrians, and tourists, prefer to experience the thrill of flying above snow by taking a tandem ride alongside an experienced "pilot." The parapente folds up into a manageable size and professional Alpinists use them as a speedy way to return home after climbing a mountain.

Bicycling has always been popular with vacationers in Austria and it is not uncommon to find bicycles for hire at a train station. In recent years more specialist mountain bicycles have been available for hire and this makes a cycle tour of the Alps more feasible than it ever was before.

Apart from the more active leisure activities many Austrians visit the health spas that are found in various parts of the country. Some of the spas are centuries old and have acquired reputations for curing or alleviating particular medical problems.

AUSTRIAN SPORTS CHAMPIONS

Soccer—Hans Krankl was the top European goal scorer in 1978 and has been voted the Sportsman of the Year five times by his fellow Austrians. He transferred to FC Barcelona and helped that team to success in the European Cup competitions.

Grand Prix Racing—Niki Lauda is one of the most famous racing car drivers ever. He won the World Championship three times, in 1975, 1977 and 1984.

Body Building—Arnold Schwarzenegger was the winner of numerous "Mister Olympia" awards before becoming even more famous after he left for Hollywood and stardom on the big screen.

SPORTSWOMAN OF THE YEAR—SEVEN TIMES!

The most successful skier in the history of the sport was a woman. Annemarie Moser-Pröll achieved her first World Cup victory at the age of 17 and went on to score another 62 World Cup victories. Silver medals at the 1972 Winter Olympics in Japan were surpassed by her performance in the 1980 Winter Olympics in Lake Placid in the United States when she won the downhill, the discipline she has always excelled in.

The only man to come close to Pröll's achievement was Franz Klammer from Carinthia. Known as "Emperor Franz," he climaxed his career at the Winter Olympic Games at Innsbruck in 1976 when he took the downhill world title.

SPANISH RIDING SCHOOL

The Spanish Riding School was founded in the 16th century to provide horses for the imperial family. Today it finances itself with shows and demonstrations of horses literally dancing. As well as pirouetting, they perform the capriole—a leap upward, with all four legs off the ground and then an outward kick of the hind legs while still in the air. The professional riders, who enter the school as apprentices as young as 17 years of age, spend five years learning how to train a horse and at least another 10 years perfecting the art of riding.

The horses, known as Lipizzaner (also spelled "Lippizaner") horses, are raised and receive their first training in the small town of Piber, in Styria, before being sent to Vienna. This breed of horse derived its name from the Austrian imperial stud at Lipizza, near Trieste, formerly a part of the Austro-Hungarian Empire. Their ancestry is Spanish, Arabian and Berber. Riders are costumed in brown uniforms with gold buttons and wear black hats with gold braiding.

These famous horses do not perform in July and August, but they can still be seen in their stables. The Spanish Riding School is directly across the street. The horses perform in the beautiful Baroque Riding Hall which was built by Fischer von Erlach in 1735. The Riding Hall was used as a ballroom during the Congress of Vienna (the epic conference in 1814 at which the great nations tried to reconstitute Europe after Napoleon's defeat).

The money earned from performances is used to buy food, the uniforms and boots. The school is economically viable because the Viennese in the past came to watch the horses every morning and were willing to pay for the performances. Now they are the most famous classical-style equestrian performers in the world.

FESTIVALS

THE FESTIVALS OF AUSTRIA are rooted in the agricultural and religious lives of the people. The two are related, for Easter time is not just a Christian festival based on the resurrection of Christ but also the birth of spring and a natural time of celebration for pastoral communities.

The least commercialized festivals in Austria are regional ones, like St. Martin's Day in Burgenland. St. Martin, the saint who shared his cloak with a poor man, is the patron saint of this province and November 11 is virtually a public holiday in this part of Austria. Geese are killed and roasted to mark the occasion. Church festivals are sometimes given their own interpretation, as on the day that commemorates Christ's final entry into Jerusalem to the cheers of the multitude who strewed his path with palm branches. In some parts of Austria, Palm Sunday is celebrated by a procession with children carrying a large bough.

The bonfires and celebrations that mark Midsummer Night across Austria have a frankly pagan origin but the event is kept alive today by rural people who are mainly Roman Catholic. Another non-religious festival is held in early summer in Weitensfeld. Called the *Kranzelreiten*, it is a kind of joust where men on horseback attempt to spear a ring. The origin of this festival dates back to the days of the plague in medieval Europe when, as a result of the epidemic, there was only one marriageable girl in the village and the three male survivors had to contend for her hand. The reward for the 20th-century winner is a *Kranzel* (wreath).

Opposite: **Dancers at the Opera Ball in Vienna.**

Below: **The Plague Memorial Column was built by Leopold I in 1679 to commemorate the end of the terrible plague.**

Other important festivals take place annually in Vienna, Burgenland, Carinthia, Linz and Bregenz. The Styrian Autumn is an avant-garde arts festival designed to prompt commendation and controversy.

A crowded street in Salzburg. Located by the river Salzach near the salt mines from which the city got its name, Salzburg is where thousands of people from all over the world come, every summer, for the Salzburg Summer Festival.

THE SALZBURG FESTIVAL

Every summer Austria hosts a variety of music festivals but the Salzburg Festival is the most famous and prestigious of them all. Max Reinhardt, the founder of the festival, was the original producer of Hofmannsthal's *Jedermann*, a version of the medieval Everyman morality play which is now a trademark of the festival. Any orchestra or opera singer invited to the festival recognizes such an invitation as a mark of international recognition. Salzburg was the home of Wolfgang Amadeus Mozart so, not surprisingly, his music is always the centerpiece.

Founded in 1920 the Festival is now a comprehensive show: theater and opera, concerts and serenades, chamber music and live street theater, recitals and lectures attract some 170,000 visitors every year. About 60% of the visitors come from abroad to Salzburg between the last week of July and the end of August.

A drama performance during the Salzburg Summer Festival.

113

CHRISTIAN FESTIVALS

At Chrismas time special carols are sung around the Christmas tableau containing figures of the the infant Jesus in a crib and the three shepherds in attendance. In many regions, the harp is still used to provide the accompanying music.

Christmas celebrations are the same across the country. Cribs are displayed in houses and on January 5 children go singing from farm to farm to mark the Three Kings' journey. Before that, on St. Nicholas's Day there are various *Christkindl* (Christchild) festivals and open-air markets selling Christmas toys and decorations. The celebrations are biggest in the town of Christkindl in Styria.

After Christmas, Easter is the most joyous Christian festival in Austria. It commemorates the resurrection of Jesus Christ and the festival blends in with ancient pagan European rites celebrating the birth of spring. Easter Sunday always falls on the Sunday after the first full moon on or following March 21. It is preceded by a period of abstinence known as Lent *(Lenz)*.

Easter Sunday is welcomed with singing, processions and music from church bells, choirs and village bands. Churches are decorated with flowers. Children receive Easter eggs brought by the Easter rabbit, vestiges of a fertility rite where the egg and rabbit symbolized fertility. The rabbit was the escort of the Germanic goddess Ostara who gave the name to the festival by way of the German *Ostern*.

An Easter ritual that is becoming less and less common is the *Schmeckostern* (Easter smacks). On Easter Monday and Tuesday men and women in parts of Austria and Germany "beat" each other with birch, cherry or vine branches in the belief that these ritual beatings bring good luck, long life and prosperity.

FESTIVAL CALENDAR

January 1: An annual concert by the Vienna Philharmonic Orchestra in Vienna; operas at the State Opera and Beethoven concert by the Vienna Symphony.

March/April: Easter Sunday.

May 30: Celebration of the Feast of Corpus Christi.

May-June: A major arts festival in Vienna. Some thousand events take place all over the city for five weeks.

June: Schubert Festival in Vorarlberg.

July-August: The Salzburg Festival and Carinthian Summer (an arts festival) are held.

Late August/Early September: the *Almabtrieb* when herders bring down their cattle from the mountain pastures for the coming winter. The cattle are formed into a procession with the leading cow festooned with ribbons.

September: Haydn Festival in Burgenland.

November 11: St. Martin's Day.

December 6: St. Nicholas, the patron saint of children, has his day and *Christkindl* festivals are held.

December 24: Midnight Mass throughout the country.

FOOD

AUSTRIAN CUISINE is a mixed one, reflecting the influences from the neighboring countries that once made up the Hapsburg Empire. Austrians eat goulash from Hungary, a bean soup from Serbia in Yugoslavia, *knödel* (bread dumpling) from Czechoslovakia and pasta dishes and ice cream from Italy. The most characteristic dish that is purely Austrian is *Wiener Schnitzel*, veal fillet lightly fried in egg and breadcrumbs. Other Austrian dishes are heavier than this, like *Tafelspitz* (boiled beef) and *Schweinsbraten* (roast pork). Cabbage soup and *Letscho* (smoked bacon stew with tomatoes and red peppers) are not so heavy.

One well-known Austrian specialty is a regional dish: the *Strudel* from Burgenland. The dough is made of flour and water with various sweet and savory fillings—apples, cottage cheese, cherries or mincemeat—enclosed in it. A specialty of Styria is *Sterz*, pork with vegetables and sweet rye bread.

Austrians start the day with not much more than coffee and a roll—a continental breakfast. A second breakfast, called *Gabelfrühsttück* (literally meaning "fork breakfast") is more substantial and resembles what hotels call an American breakfast. For a mid-afternoon break Austrians enjoy *Jause*, which consists of something light with coffee.

Opposite: Mozartkugeln candy makers display their creations which look almost too good to eat.

Below: A café—a good place for an inexpensive meal and a good cup of coffee.

EATING PLACES

On the street can be found the *Würstelstand* (sausage merchant), the nearest thing to a hot dog stand in Austria. Working people will pop into the *Imbisstube* or *Gasthäuser*—simple snack bars or informal restaurants. More expensive, but still less formal and less costly than the hotel restaurants, are the various wine cellars and wine gardens that now serve snacks, buffet lunches and dinners. Although the wine cellars started out just serving wine, groups of friends or families are now visiting them more for the food than the drink.

Austrian etiquette as regards eating and dining often appears rather formal to outsiders. Where Americans would happily use their hands when eating a sandwich, Austrians are just as likely to use a knife and fork. Expensive restaurants often expect their customers to wear a jacket and tie and in Vienna even moderately priced restaurants prefer diners to wear formal dress. The general rule that is often given to foreigners and tourists is: when in doubt—dress up!

THE PASTRY SHOP

The Austrians' love of good food is best represented by the tempting array of pastries to be found in the *Konditorei*, a specialized version of the coffee house selling tarts, fritters and sweets. The *Konditorei* is filled with small tables where the pastry is served with coffee or hot chocolate.

A take-out service is always available and the choice of pastries and confectionaries can be very tempting:

- *Palatschinken*—pancakes stuffed with sweet or savory fillings.
- *Zwetschkenknödel*—a sweet made of damson plums with the stones replaced by lumps of sugar and the whole fruit covered with a light dumpling.
- *Kaiserschmarren*—this is translated as "emperor's omelette." It is a pancake of sorts cut up and mixed with jam or fruit and covered with a thin dusting of sugar.
- *Sachertorte*—jam cake iced with chocolate.
- *Gugelhupf*—sponge cake.

Opposite top: **A restaurant menu beckons the hungry. There are meals which can be obtained for very moderate prices in certain eating places.**

Opposite bottom: **A shop selling sausages and meat; sausages are eaten with** *Sauerkraut* **and dumplings and washed down with some beer.**

Left: **A bakery with different types of bread.**

119

Many small vineyards can be found in certain stretches of the Danube Valley, producing new wines for consumption locally.

"We give every man the freedom to sell or dispense —all year and at any time, any price and in any form—food and wine that he has produced himself."
— Emperor Joseph II , August 17, 1784

WINE

The traditional image of dark wine cellars with countless racks of wine gathering dust as they mature over the years does not really apply to Austria. The country's wines are characteristically light and require little maturing. This is the origin of the *Heurige* which serve the fresh new wine of the year. Connoisseurs usually follow a couple of glasses of the new wine with some of the older wine.

Compared to France and Germany, the wines of Austria are not that famous. The regions serve local wines that never reach the supermarkets and this is particularly true of the wines from Burgenland. The better-known wines come from southern Tyrol and Lower Austria, away from the main Alps.

Small vineyards are very common around Vienna and eastern Austria. Toward the end of the 18th century the emperor issued a decree that precipitated the rapid development of small family vineyards and many of those producing wine today can trace their history back to that time.

COFFEE IN VIENNA

Coffee was introduced to Austria unintentionally more than 400 years ago by the Turks. Coffee was much in use by the Moslems because alcohol was taboo to them. However, coffee was not yet known in Europe. Like tea to the British, coffee soon became an important beverage to the Austrian people after an enterprising Austrian merchant experimented with the brew.

The Viennese in particular have brought coffee drinking to a fine art. They have created more than 20 varieties of coffee. Some of the varieties include:

- *Mokka*—small cups of black coffee with sugar.
- *Kaffee mit Schlag*—coffee with whipped cream.
- *Doppelschlag*—coffee with a double portion of whipped cream.
- *Einspänner*—literally translates as "a one-horse coach," meaning a glass of coffee topped with whipped cream.
- *Türkischer*—black coffee boiled in a copper pot and served in tiny cups.

There are many other varieties of coffee but one thing is always the same—the coffee that is ordered will always be accompanied by a glass of water piped in from the Alps. Nobody really knows why water is always served as well. Some explain that it is part of Austrian hospitality and courtesy, others explain that because the taste of coffee is so strong, a sip of water is necessary to clear the taste.

Apart from coffee and wine, beer is another favorite Austrian drink.

REGIONAL FOOD

In the Alpine regions a favorite hot dish, especially among skiers who have just come in from the cold, is a bowl of *Leberknödelsuppe* (chicken liver dumplings). A lighter dish would be a plate of *Speck* (smoked bacon and cheese).

A café in a mountain resort. Skiers warm themselves up after being in the cold with some piping hot food.

Goulash is the Hungarian dish that is most commonly eaten in Austria. It is a soup that can easily become a whole meal in itself and it often appears as such on Austrian menus. Ingredients can include green peppers, tomatoes, onions, beef or perhaps pork and the obligatory paprika. Goulash is not spicy in taste and does not, contrary to what a lot of people think, contain sour cream.

Fondue is another dish that is not Austrian but eaten by the Austrians. It is actually a Swiss national dish of melted cheeses. White wine is first heated in a heavy casserole that has been rubbed with garlic. Then grated cheese is added to the hot wine with some cornstarch and a dash of nutmeg for flavor. The fondue is eaten communally, straight from the pot. Diners are provided with cubes of crusty bread, which they spear on long-handled forks and dip into the hot mixture.

THE IMPORTANCE OF FOOD

In the state of Tyrol, the importance of food is reflected in folktales and festivals. This may have to do with the fact that during the cold winter there was no food easily available and survival depended entirely on a family's ability to prepare for the winter months during the summer and fall. The wasting of food was thus seen as an unforgivable sin. Frau Hütt is a Tyrolean folktale character who did waste food and was consequently turned into stone for doing so.

The importance of food is also seen in the way All Souls' Day is still sometimes observed in Tyrol. All Souls' Day commemorates the souls of the dead and the belief that those souls not yet purified for heaven may be aided by prayer. In parts of Tyrol and northern Italy this is linked to a belief that the dead may return on that day and so strong is the belief that food is left out overnight on the kitchen table for them.

Winters are harsh in the mountainous regions and being prepared for the worst is vitally important. Food is salted and smoked, while fire wood is chopped and stacked ready for use.

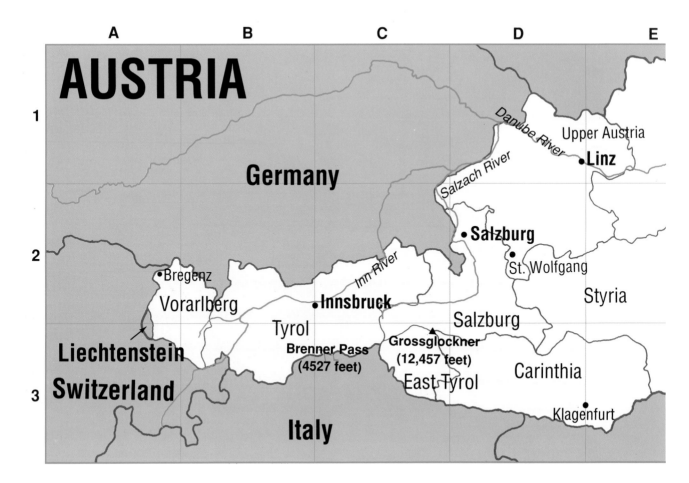

AUSTRIA

Germany

Danube River

Upper Austria

•Linz

Salzach River

•Salzburg

St. Wolfgang

Styria

Inn River

•Bregenz

Vorarlberg

•Innsbruck

Tyrol

Brenner Pass
(4527 feet)

Salzburg

Grossglockner
(12,457 feet)

East Tyrol

Carinthia

Liechtenstein

Switzerland

Klagenfurt

Italy

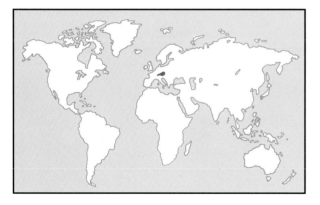

International Boundary
State Boundary
▲ Mountain
● Capital
● City
River
Lake

QUICK NOTES

LAND AREA
32,376 square miles

POPULATION
7.5 million

CAPITAL
Vienna

MAJOR CITIES
Graz, Linz, Salzburg, Innsbruck

CLIMATE
Temperate, varies with elevation

LONGEST RIVER
Danube (1,770 miles)

HIGHEST POINT
Grossglockner (12,457 feet)

NATIONAL ANTHEM
Österreichische Bundeshymne
(Opening line translates as: Land of mountains, land of rivers.)

OFFICIAL LANGUAGE
German

NEIGHBORING COUNTRIES
Germany and Czechoslovakia (in the north)
Hungary (in the east)
Yugoslavia and Italy (in the south)
Switzerland and Liechtenstein (in the west)

MAJOR RELIGION
Roman Catholic

CURRENCY
Schilling
100 groschen = 1 schilling
US$1 = 12.29 schillings

MEASUREMENTS
Metric system

ECONOMY
Lumber, chemicals, mining, hydroelectric power, textiles, tourism

LEADERS IN POLITICS
Adolf Hitler—the dictator of Germany from 1933 to 1945. Born and raised in Austria.
Kurt Waldheim—General Secretary of the United Nations and President of Austria between 1986 and 1992.
Franz Vranitzky—the Chancellor of Austria and leader of the Socialist Party, the leader group in the coalition governing Austria.

FAMOUS AUSTRIAN MUSICIANS
Joseph Haydn
Wolfgang Amadeus Mozart
Franz Schubert
Johann Strauss Sr. and Jr.
Arnold Schönberg

OTHER FAMOUS AUSTRIANS
Sigmund Freud (Psychology)
Ludwig Wittgenstein (Philosophy)
Oskar Kokoschka (Painting)
Arnold Schwarzenegger (Body builder and film star)

GLOSSARY

Gemütlichkeit	An attitude which creates a leisurely, warm and friendly atmosphere, full of cosiness, geniality and joviality.
Langlauf	Cross-country skiing.
plebiscite	A vote by which people of a political unit determine autonomy or affiliation with another country.
Ringstrasse	The circuit thoroughfare around Vienna.
Schloss	A residence of the Austrian nobility.
Strudel	Light pastry filled with sweet or savory fillings.
The Social Partnership	The convention whereby leaders of the employers and trade unions meet to seek a compromise on wages and prices.
waltz	A three-step dance, characterized by slow formal steps.
Wiener Schnitzel	Veal fillet fried in egg and breadcrumbs.

BIBLIOGRAPHY

Austrian National Tourist Office: 545 Fifth Avenue, New York, NY 10036.
Greene, Carol: *Austria*, Childrens Press, Chicago, 1986.
Hadley, L.: *Fielding's Europe With Children*, William Morrow, New York, 1984.
Lye, Keith: *Take a Trip to Austria*, Franklin Watts, New York, 1987.
Lye, Keith (editor): *Today's World—Europe*, Gloucester Press, New York, 1987.
Matthews III, William H.: *The Story of Glaciers and the Ice Age*, Harvey House, New York, 1974.
National Geographic: *Picture Atlas of Our World*, National Geographic Society, Washington D.C., 1980.
Ventura, Piero: *Great Composers*, G.P. Putnam's Sons, New York, 1989.

INDEX

PICTURE CREDITS
Andre Laubier Picture Library: 14, 21, 22, 55, 95, 97, 98, 120
Austrian Tourist Promotion Board: 1, 5, 7, 16, 36, 38, 40, 69, 75, 107, 109, 110, 113, 125, back cover
Helmut Kaltner: 73
Image Bank: Front cover, 8, 24, 26, 29, 30, 35, 48, 61, 62, 116
K.F. Seetoh: 4, 44, 52, 53, 56, 59, 63, 65, 71, 81, 85, 86, 92, 93, 96, 99, 117
Les Voyageurs: 18, 27, 72, 78, 87, 98, 101
Life File Photographic Library: 9, 11, 12, 15, 17, 19, 20, 23, 28, 31, 32, 34, 39, 40, 43, 45, 46, 47, 50, 57, 58, 60, 64, 66, 67, 68, 70, 74, 76, 77, 79, 80, 82, 83, 88, 90, 91, 94, 102, 103, 104, 105, 106, 111, 112, 115, 118, 119, 121, 122, 123